FEARFUL CROSSING

ISBN 0-913814-85-7

This book was originally published by Great
Basin Press in 1982. First revised edition
by Nevada Publications was published in 1987.

Proudly printed in the United States of America

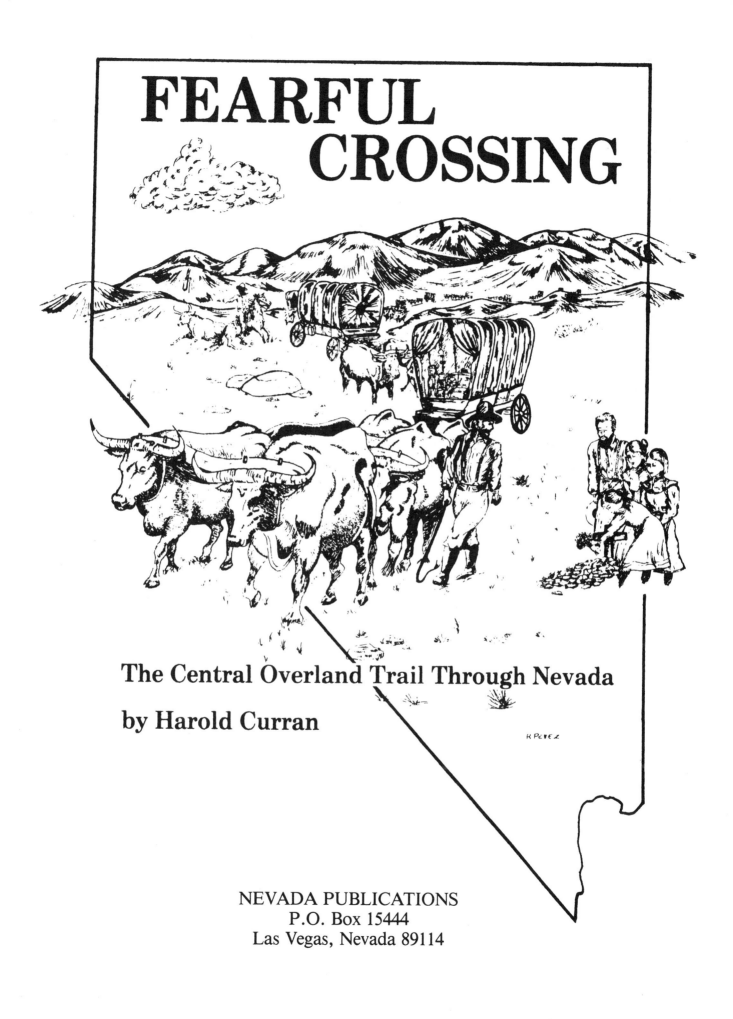

FEARFUL CROSSING

The Central Overland Trail Through Nevada

by Harold Curran

NEVADA PUBLICATIONS
P.O. Box 15444
Las Vegas, Nevada 89114

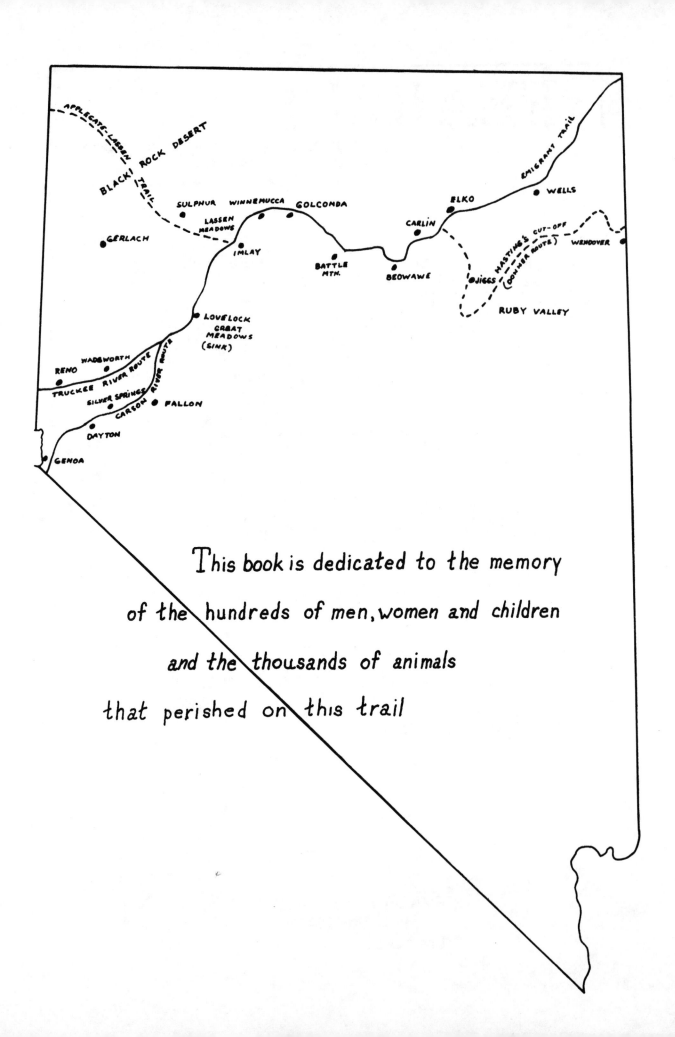

This book is dedicated to the memory
of the hundreds of men, women and children
and the thousands of animals
that perished on this trail

Contents

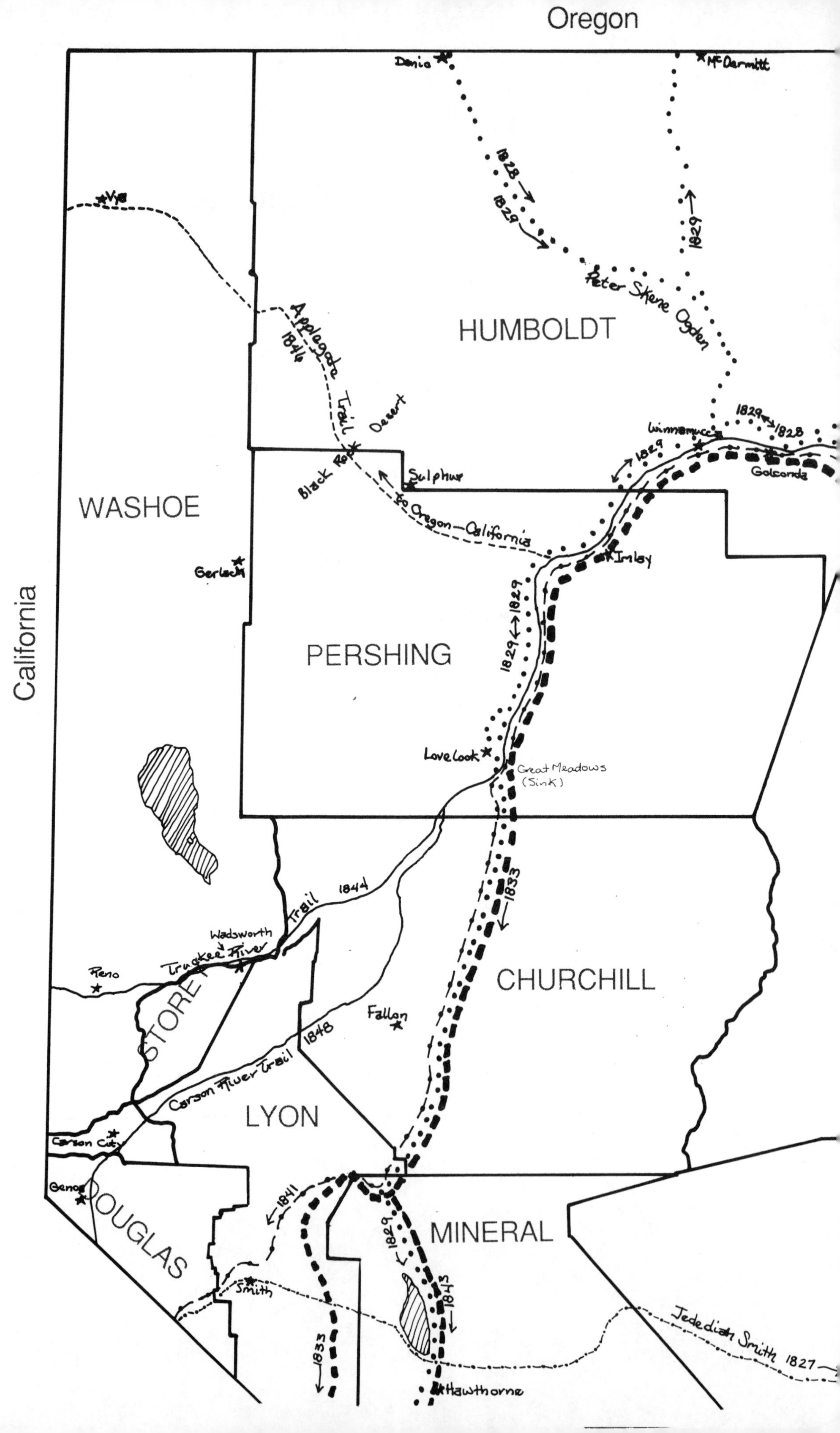

Oregon

Denio ★

★ McDarmitt

1828

1829

Peter Skene Ogden

HUMBOLDT

Applegate Trail
1846

Desert

Black Rock ★

Sulphur

To Oregon–California

1829 ← 1828

Winnemucca ★

1829

Golconda

WASHOE

Gerlach ★

PERSHING

1829 ← 1829

Imlay ★

Love Lock ★

Great Meadows
(Sink)

Trail

1844

Wadsworth

Truckee River

Reno ★

STOREY

Fallon ★

1848

Carson River Trail

LYON

1833

CHURCHILL

Carson City ★

Genoa ★

DOUGLAS

1841

1829

MINERAL

Smith ★

1843

Jedediah Smith 1827

1833

★ Hawthorne

California

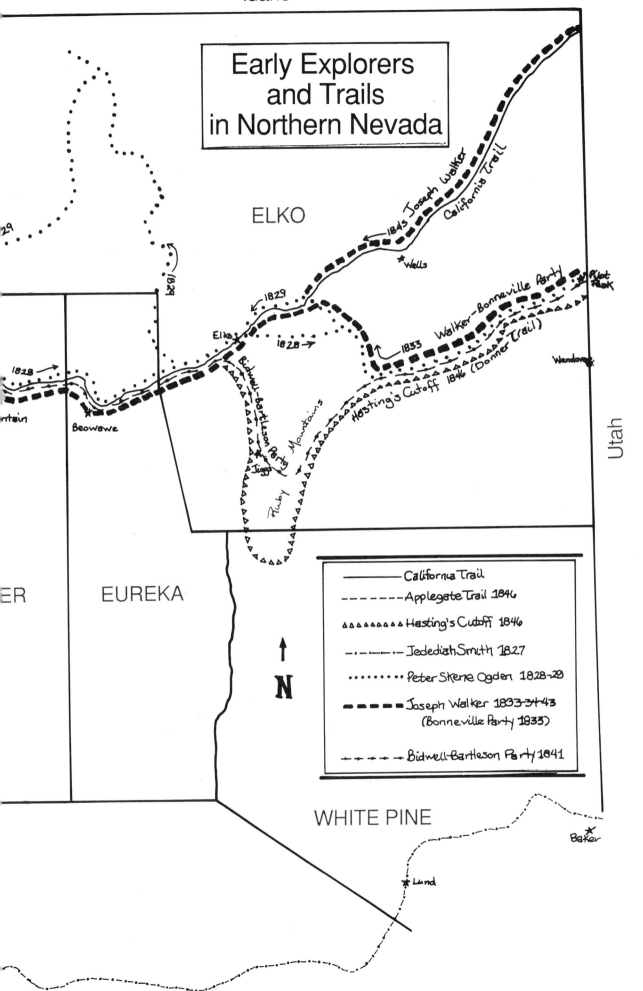

Preface

This book is about the crossing of Nevada by the overland emigrants, from their entry on the eastern boundary to just beyond their departure in the west, where they traversed California's Sierra Nevada. It demonstrates how the geography of Nevada was an important factor in the development of the western section of this nation, for the state was so strategically located that it became a challenge and a formidable foe to those trying to cross it.

I am aware that public school students studying Nevada history learn about the emigrants. However, reading material on the subject is often either not available, or too complicated for them. It is my sincere hope that the material in this book will provide needed information and be interesting. It is also hoped that the average adult will find the book interesting and even the serious reader on the emigrants will find some new material and observations.

A considerable amount of time is devoted to discussing the Humboldt River and travel down its valley, because this stream was the main artery of the trail. The emigrants spent two thirds of their time in the valley of the Humboldt while crossing Nevada.

The only trails considered at length in this writing are the principal ones, those that were established in the 1840's and became main routes of travel. Shortly after 1850 numerous new trails were opened off these early major routes. Noble's Road branched off the Applegate Trail; the Beckwourth Pass, the Henness Pass and the Auburn Emigrant Road branched off the Truckee River Route. A trail to Calaveras County was opened from the Carson River Route. The purpose of this work would not be furthered by including detailed discussions of these later and less important trails.

The Donner Party is referred to in different parts of the work because the group is well-known and because it was felt that such coverage is necessary to inform the reader of the general route the Donners took in crossing Nevada. One may then be able to realize the difficulties the members of the party encountered even before they reached the snow-covered mountains. No attempt is made to go into detail about their hardships.

Many hours were spent doing research in libraries and in the field before any conclusions were made. Quotations taken from the emigrants' diaries are used to support statements or to emphasize points and give reality to the subject, so that the story of the crossing is told largely in the words of the emigrants. Many of the emigrants had little formal education or were foreigners and in their diaries words were spelled as they sounded to the writers; there has been no attempt to make corrections.

The pictures are all recent ones, taken by the writer in the hope that they would complement and clarify the narrative for readers.

I had no intention of ever writing a book, but have been interested in the emigrants' crossing of Nevada because it is a fascinating subject. The reading of many diaries brought a revelation of the struggle and the hardships that the emigrants experienced, and a new appreciation of their accomplishments. I can now see the Humboldt River and its valley in a perspective entirely different from that in which they are viewed by today's travelers.

There are some people with a lot of knowledge about the trail and the emigrants. Most of them have very set ideas on these subjects and do not agree amongst themselves on many points. If this writer has written anything that anyone disagrees with, I hope that person will extend to me the same courtesy of respect for individual thinking and opinion that I extend to him.

My sincere thanks are extended to Nevada Wheeler and Virginia Phillips for reading the manuscript and making grammatical corrections. To Rudy Perez of Fallon many thanks for the drawing of the emigrant train on the cover and the mountains on the maps. I extend my sincere appreciation to Ray Bedke and his family of Oakley, Idaho, for the courtesies I received from them. To those people in the Special Collections Department of the University of Nevada-Reno Library and at the Nevada Historical Society I extend my deepest appreciation. I wish to thank, especially, Lee Mortensen who has been most helpful in providing me with information. Dr. Everett Harris, who is not only a good friend but a knowledgeable trail man, has been of inestimable help in every possible way. He has given unselfishly of his time and knowledge and, most importantly, has offered encouragement.

To all these people, again - thanks.

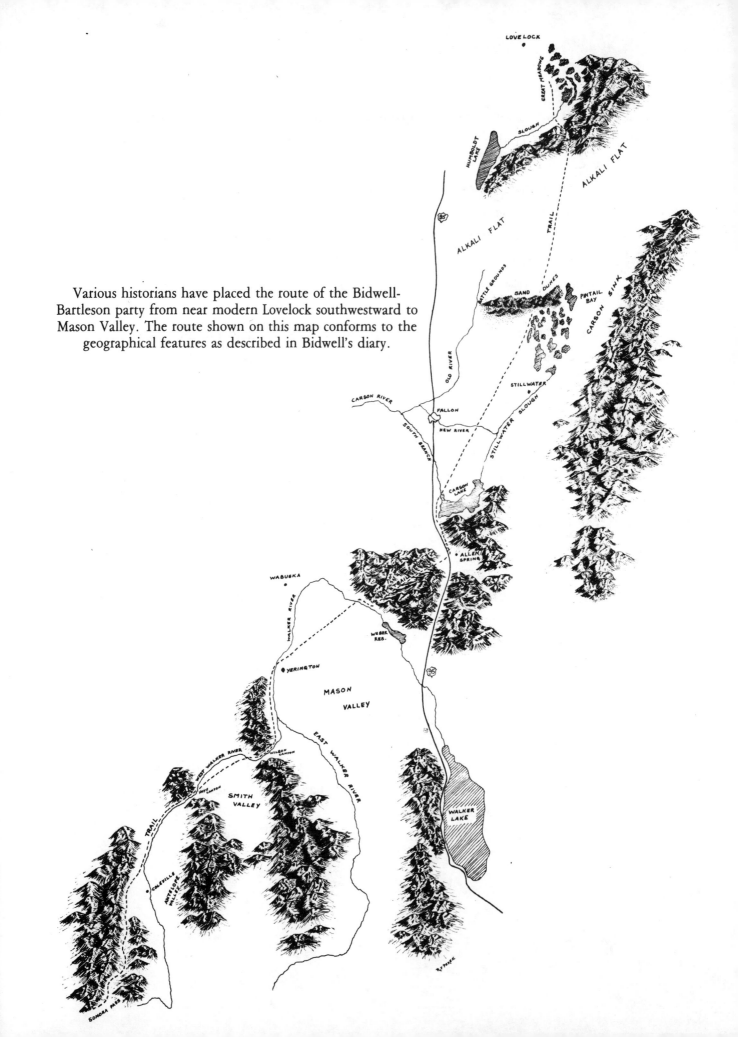

Various historians have placed the route of the Bidwell-Bartleson party from near modern Lovelock southwestward to Mason Valley. The route shown on this map conforms to the geographical features as described in Bidwell's diary.

AN EMIGRANT CAMP.

David Rohrer Leeper

*Reprinted illustrations and the quotations in
the text are keyed to the bibliography.*

I. Background: The Development of the Trail

The American people have always turned their eyes toward the west.
From the Atlantic coast they crossed the Appalachian Mountains into Kentucky,
Tennessee, and the Ohio Valley. This thousand mile advance, over some two
hundred years, was halted at the Mississippi River. Beyond its broad waters
lay the colonial domains of France, England, Spain, and Russia.

The American tide could be stemmed only momentarily, however. Political
leaders like Thomas Jefferson were already eyeing the Pacific coast and popular
pressure for expansion into new lands was great. When Napoleon, his wars
going badly, offered the United States all the land claimed by France between
the Mississippi River and the Rocky Mountains, the offer was readily accepted.
This 1803 "Louisiana Purchase" opened vast new areas to Americans - among
them the mountain men, who could then legally roam the Rockies in quest of furs.

These courageous trappers and traders expanded American knowledge of
the west, always exploring what was just beyond the next range of mountains.
Each further western penetration added information about the huge unknown
country and, in turn, kindled more curiosity. The Franciscan Fathers Dominguez
and Escalante had already been in part of that country, and other missionaries
like Jason and Daniel Lee, Henry Spaulding, and Marcus Whitman also contributed
to the great western expansion. However, it was the mountain men such as John
Colter, Jedediah Smith, Nathaniel Wyeth, Jim Bridger, Joseph Walker, Kit Carson,
Thomas Fitzpatrick, and James Clyman who did most of the exploring and opened
the trails.

In 1807, one of these mountain men, John Colter, could not restrain his
curiosity and started west by himself. He roamed through land that no other
white man had seen and he beheld wonders of nature that were almost unbelievable,
including what is now Yellowstone National Park. When he returned, his stories
of what he had seen further stimulated the exploring urge in other mountain men.

In 1826, Jedediah Smith and a party of trappers started for California.
They traveled by a southern route down the Colorado River and across the Mojave
Desert. The following spring, Smith attempted to cross the Sierra Nevada from
California on his return to the annual rendezvous of the mountain men. His first
attempts to cross the mountains failed because of the deep snow; but finally, in

the vicinity of Ebbetts Pass, he crossed with two men. These were the first white men to cross the Sierra, as far as we know.

Traveling east in Nevada, Smith was near the south shore of Walker Lake June 1, 1827. He spent one night here and quickly moved on, as his main objective was to get to the rendezvous at Bear Lake, Utah as soon as possible. While crossing the desolate and barren expanse of central Nevada, he and his men suffered from a lack of water and food, but they arrived at the rendezvous on time. Ten days after his arrival, he again headed back to California to rejoin the men he had left there. He followed his previous route down the Colorado River and had a disasterous encounter with Indians, but he made it back to his men.

Jedediah Smith is often credited with being the first white man in Nevada, although Peter Skene Ogden may have crossed the northern boundary for a short distance in 1826, a few months before Smith's entry, and the Spanish priest Francisco Garces may have traveled through extreme southern Nevada in 1776. None of these entries contributed anything to the development of the trail through the state. This accomplishment was to be left to the exploring expedition that entered Nevada a year after Smith left.

Peter Skene Ogden, a Canadian in the employ of the British Hudson's Bay Company, followed Smith into Nevada on what was the second appreciable penetration into the territory. Ogden and his party of trappers entered Nevada on its northern boundary late in 1828, and traveled down the Little Humboldt River until they discovered the Humboldt River itself near Winnemucca. They trapped for a while at that location; but as winter was near and game on the river was scarce, Ogden decided to head east and winter in buffalo country. He and his party traveled up the Humboldt River past Elko, left the river at a point near Halleck, went through Secret Pass, and continued east past Montello to their winter camp.

The following spring Ogden returned to the Humboldt River and trapped it down to its end, near Lovelock, Nevada. He then traveled back up the river to where he had discovered it the year before. Here he left it and returned to the Hudson Bay quarters at Fort Nez Perces on the Columbia River.

Four months after his departure from the Humboldt River Ogden was back again to explore further to the south. The record of this journey through Nevada, down the Colorado River, and back up through California to his headquarters was lost when he crossed the Columbia River. Gloria Griffin Cline, who has made extensive studies on Ogden, states:

> *From the Sink [they] struck south and southwestward into previously unexplored terrain, undoubtedly passing from the Humboldt Sink to the Carson Sink and on to the Walker River, which the group followed down to Walker Lake; thus the comment in Ogden's letter: "six days after discovered a fine large river but destitute of Beaver." From Walker Lake the party continued in a southwestwardly direction moving out into the barren Great Basin terrain which lies to the south of the present Nevada city of Hawthorne. . .*

On the basis of this quotation, Ogden would be the second white man to visit Walker Lake (being preceded by Jedediah Smith). The paths of these two great trappers and explorers crossed here in Nevada near the south end of Walker Lake; Smith traveling from west to east and Ogden from north to south.

The next two groups into Nevada, the Walker-Bonneville party and the Bidwell-Bartleson party, probably followed Ogden's route to the Walker River. Ogden's expedition to the south contributed very little to the development of the trail, but his discovery of the Humboldt River was of real significance, as that stream became the backbone of the trail.

The Humboldt was known by many names, some of them unprintable. Ogden himself called it the "Unknown River" and his men called it "Paul's River", in memory of one of the trappers who died on it. Others called it "Ogden's River." Ogden said it probably should be named the "Swampy River" because a stranger passing this way would recognize it by that name, but the river was known to most emigrants as "Mary's" or "St. Mary's River" until Fremont changed the name to Humboldt River. It has been said that it was the most hated and yet the most necessary river in America. The mountain ranges in Nevada run north and south, yet this river found its way west to form a passageway for the thousands of emigrants who were to follow its winding course.

In 1833, the mountain men held their rendezvous in the Green River Valley. The well-known Joseph Walker was there and organized a party of about sixty men to head west. Although it was not explicitly stated, California was obviously their destination. Walker had been employed by Captain Benjamin Louis Eulalie de Bonneville, a West Point graduate on leave from the United States Army. The party became known as the Bonneville party. Was it a

15

trapping or an exploring expedition for military information? The answer to this question, as well as the route they followed across Nevada and over the mountains, remain unknown. Zenas Leonard was appointed clerk of the expedition.

After leaving the rendezvous the party traveled around the north shore of Salt Lake and entered Nevada on the east at Pilot Peak, which Leonard describes:

> *After traveling a few days longer thro these barren plains; we came to the mountain described by the Indian as having its peak covered with snow. It presents a most singular appearance - being entirely unconnected with any other chain. It is surrounded on either side by level plain, and rises abruptly to a great heighth, rugged and hard to ascend. To take a view of the surrounding country from the mountain, the eye meets nothing but a smooth sandy, level plain.*

The party continued westwardly in Nevada and probably used Secret Pass, as Ogden had done, to come to the Humboldt River:

> *At this place, all the branches of this stream is collected from the mountains into the main channel, which forms quite a large stream; and to which we gave the name of Barren River - a name which we thought would be quite appropraite, as the Country, natives, and every thing belonging to it, justly deserves the name. - You may travel for many days on the banks of this river, without finding a stick large enough to make a walking cane.*

Here they began trapping for beaver and the Indians stole some of their traps. In retaliation the trappers killed some Indians. The number killed and the manner in which they were killed is debated, but the incident created a hatred among the Indians for this group. Leonard recounts the confrontation:

> *So eager were they to posses themselves of our traps, that we were forced to quit trapping in this vicinity and make for some other quarter. The great annoyance we sustained in this respect greatly displeased some of our men, and they were for taking vengence before we left the country - but this was not the disposition of Captain Walker. These discontents being out hunting one day, fell in with a few Indians, two or three of whom they killed, and then returning to camp, not daring to let the Captain know it. The next day while hunting, they repeated the same violation - but this time not quite so successful, for the Captain found it out, and immediately took measures for its effectual suppression.*

Walker and his party continued down the Humboldt River until it ended near Lovelock, Nevada. The Indians had sent ahead word of the killings on the upper part of the river, and Walker was confronted there by a large number of them. These Indians had only bows and arrows and did not attack Walker's group, but taunted them to the point that Walker ordered an attack. The Indians were not familiar with guns and did not realize how powerful they were. Before the order to attack was given Walker demonstrated the power of the guns by having some of his men shoot and kill some ducks in a nearby pond. The Indians then put up a beaver skin as a target and Walker's men shot at it to convince them that the guns could be harmful. When the Indians were not impressed and continued to be bothersome, the attack was made:

> We closed in on them and fired, leaving thirty-nine
> dead on the field - which was nearly half - the remainder
> were overwhelmed with dismay - running into the high
> grass in every direction; howling in the most lamentable
> manner.

Walker's route to this point is fairly definite, but from here on it is a matter of conjecture as to where he went. Leonard says:

> We left these Indians and built rafts out of rushes
> to convey us across the river, when we left the Lakes
> and continued our course in the direction of a large
> mountain, which was in sight, and which we could see
> was covered with snow on the summit. In the evening
> we camped on the margin of a large Lake formed by a
> river which heads in this mountain. This Lake,
> likewise, has no outlet for the water, except that
> which sinks into the ground. The water in this Lake is
> similar to lie, and tastes much like pearlash.

The mountain described seems to be Mt. Grant by Walker Lake. From the north it can be seen for many miles. The lake must have been Carson Lake, southeast of present Fallon, Nevada, but the mention of the river is very confusing. Adding to the confusion, Leonard continues: "The next day we traveled up this river toward the mountain; where we encamped for the night." If they camped on Carson Lake, and traveled up the river that flowed into it, they would have followed the South Branch of the Carson River to the main river and then moved in a westerly direction to Carson Valley. Francis Farquhar, in his *History of the Sierra Nevada,* states: "We may assume that the party came to Carson Valley." However, this assumption is hard to accept because there is no evidence they reached the valley.

The Bonneville party was composed of experienced mountain men who were accustomed to finding their way through mountain passes and following rivers and streams. If they had reached Carson Valley by following the Carson River, they surely would have found one of the passes near the valley - and would not have ended up wandering around in the mountains by Yosemite Valley far to the south. The East and West Carson Rivers meet in Carson Valley near Genoa. If Walker's group had followed the West Carson River, it would have taken them over Kit Carson Pass, the same route that most of the later emigrants followed. If, for some reason, they had taken the East Carson River, it would have led them high into rugged mountains, where they probably would have found either Ebbetts or Sonora Pass. It is not logical that Walker and his men followed the Carson River. One way or another they must have ended up on the Walker River that flows into Walker Lake.

The mountain men exchanged knowledge and experiences with each other, and certainly Walker had heard of Ogden's journey three and a half years before. One or more of the free trappers with Walker may have been with Ogden and showed Walker the earlier route. There was also a well-beaten Indian trail from Carson Lake to Walker Lake as noted by Nicholas Dawson, a writer in the later Bidwell-Bartleson party:

> There was a plain trail, which we were following. . .
> After fording the stream that flowed into this
> Lake. . . went ahead on the trail. . . Crossing
> a ridge we came in sight of another Lake.

If Walker's party did follow the Indian trail, or Ogden's trail, they would have gone to Walker Lake and then up the Walker River. In Mason Valley, near the town of Yerington, they would have come to the junction of the East and West Walker Rivers. The West Walker would have been the logical one to follow, and would have taken them to the Sierra Nevada near Coleville, California. There they could either have left the river and headed into the mountains, or continued to follow it into Pickle Meadows, Leavitt Meadows and over Sonora Pass. However, they did not go over this pass, so why did they end up so much further south, at Yosemite?

The East Walker River would have taken them near Bridgeport, California and closer to Yosemite Valley, but these experienced mountain men would probably not have chosen this branch of the river over the west branch. The only thing that is certain about their travels is that they ended up on the heights above Yosemite Valley and crossed the mountains from this point. Walker wanted to be remembered as the one who discovered Yosemite and by his request it is engraved upon his tombstone - "Camped at Yosemite - Nov. 13, 1833." Since the direction of their travels in this section of the country remains a mystery, this writer will add to the confusion and suggest that Walker, if he were following Ogden's trail, might have continued south from Walker Lake and then turned west toward the mountains. This course could easily have brought him near Bridgeport, California, and closer to Yosemite.

In 1834 Walker began his return trip from California. He traveled south along the Sierra until he found an easy pass at the southern end. This is now known as Walker Pass. He traveled through the pass to the east side of the Sierra Nevada and then headed north to find his trail of the previous year. Again Leonard's narrative is very confusing, but Walker and his party did wander into a desert country and suffer from a lack of water, as Leonard states:

> It is true, we had food, but our thirst far exceeded
> any description. At last it became so intense, that
> whenever one of our cattle or horses would die the
> men would immediately catch the blood and greedily
> swallow it down.

On this desert they lost sixty-four horses, ten cows and fifteen dogs. The dogs were a source of food, as dog meat was considered a delicacy among the mountain men.

They finally found the trail they used going to California and followed it to the meadows where the Humboldt River ends. Here, again, they had trouble with the Indians. In a skirmish more Indians were killed:

> Being thus compelled to fight, as we thought, in a good
> cause and in self defence, we drew up in battle array,
> and fell on the Indians in the wildest and most ferocious
> manner we could, killing 14, besides wounding a great
> many more as we rode right over them.

After the fight the party followed the Humboldt River up to its beginning and then headed to the Snake River and game country.

There is no doubt that there were in Walker's party some men who had an intense hatred for Indians and delighted in killing them. The trappers must have committed some atrocious acts on the upper part of the river to arouse these Indians as they did. The Indians living along the Humboldt River were not warriors and had only the simplest kind of weapons. They would steal but could not be considered dangerous to this well-armed group of mountain men. Peter Skene Ogden had traveled up and down the river without any conflict with them and there is no doubt that Capt. Walker did not condone the actions taken by some of his men on the river.

Walker's party traveled the whole course of the Humboldt River and established a route for future emigrants to follow through most of Nevada. They left unanswered questions as to the real purpose of their journey, however, since very little time was spent trapping. Why did the group have so much trouble with the Indians and was the killing of so many justifiable? Where did they travel after leaving the end of the Humboldt River? Why is Walker Lake not mentioned on either their trip to California or the return, when they most definitely went by Walker Lake? Zenas Leonard, as the clerk, should have made a more exact record of the travels and the country. His narrative was published in 1839, so it was written in a reasonable time after his return, yet it is very confusing and not trustworthy.

Regardless of any unanswered questions, the stories these men would tell about the western land, and especially about a river that could be followed for three hundred miles, would stir the imagination and encourage others. Walker's journey was a major stepping stone in the development of the trail.

Once the mountain men had been to California and a river had been discovered that flowed westward in the Great Basin, the time had come for emigrants in wagon trains to attempt the journey to the Pacific Coast. In May of 1841, about fifty emigrants assembled at Sapling Grove, Missouri, near the Missouri River. Their destination was California. The members of the party elected John Bartleson to be their captain and became known as the Bartleson party. The group would also be called the Bidwell-Bartleson party, when one of its organizers, schoolteacher John Bidwell, assumed a leadership position. The emigrants had no guide and knew very little about the country they would be crossing. Fortunately, a party of missionaries was starting out for Oregon at the same time. The missionaries were headed by the Jesuit priest Pierre Jean DeSmet and had as their pilot the well-known mountain man Thomas "Broken Hand" Fitzpatrick. The emigrants joined the missionaries and thus were assured of guidance on the trail as far as they wanted to go toward Oregon.

Shortly before reaching Fort Hall, in present-day Idaho, most of the emigrants left the Oregon Trail and set out in a westerly direction toward California. The remainder of the original Bidwell-Bartleson party decided to continue on to Oregon. Thirty-two men, one woman, and a child were left in the party bound for California, with Benjamin Kelsey, his wife, Nancy, and their infant daughter, Ann, making up the only family. The group was small, but its importance was great, for it was the first to attempt to take wagons to California by the central overland route.

The Bidwell-Bartleson party, journeying determinedly into an unknown land, also epitomized the courage and spirit of thousands of emigrants who traveled overland. This is especially true of the indomitable eighteen-year-old Nancy Kelsey, who stated, "Where my husband goes, I go. I can better endure the hardships of the journey, than the anxieties for an absent husband." She and her child were the first white females to cross Nevada and the Sierra Nevada.

After leaving the Oregon-bound emigrants, the Bidwell-Bartleson party traveled to the north of Great Salt Lake and finally entered Nevada near Pilot Peak, southeast of the town of Wells, Nevada. They were now on about the same trail that Peter Skene Ogden had used thirteen years before and that Joseph Walker, with the Bonneville party, had used eight years earlier. After crossing the present eastern boundary of Nevada they traveled in a westerly direction through Silver Zone Pass toward the Pequop Mountains and camped at the present Big Springs Ranch. Here they decided to leave the wagons and pack the rest of the way, as Bidwell recounted:

> Started very early, day was exceedingly warm, passed
> through a gap in a ridge of mountains, came into a
> high dry plain, traveled some distance into it, saw
> the form of a high mountain through the smoky
> atmosphere - reached it, having come about 15 miles -
> found plenty of water - our animals were nearly given
> out. We were obliged to go so much further, in order
> to get along with the wagons. We concluded to leave
> them and pack as many things as we could.

They had brought the wagons approximately twenty five miles into Nevada.

Five years later, George McKinstry, who carried a copy of Bidwell's diary, camped at these springs and made the following notation:

> *We camped at this spring Monday July 6th 1846. And*
> *we cooked our supper & breakfast with fires made*
> *from the remains of three wagons.*

The historical significance of the Bidwell-Bartleson party was diminished after they abandoned their wagons and became a pack train. However, they were still the first group of emigrants to cross to California by the central overland route.

Leaving the springs they crossed the Pequop Mountains, probably using a pass north of Jasper Pass, which was later used by Hastings and the Donner party, and then continued in a westerly direction to the East Humboldt Mountains. Here they were within a short distance and easy travel of that which they were seeking - the headwaters of Mary's River (Humboldt River). Unfortunately, they turned south instead of north and crossed the East Humboldt Mountains into Ruby Valley:

> *Passed along one of the highest mountains we had seen*
> *in our whole journey, seeking a place to scale it, as*
> *we wished to travel W. instead of S. being convinced,*
> *that we were already far enough South. At length*
> *passed through and descended into a beautiful valley,*
> *inclining towards the W. All now felt confident that*
> *we were close on the head waters of Mary's river -*
> *distance 25 miles. Two hunters slept out last night,*
> *the company taking a different direction from that*
> *which they expected.*

Then they passed the hot springs:

> *Hunters returned: many Antelope were seen and 2 or 3*
> *killed. About 10 o'clock A.M. as we were coasting*
> *along the mountain in a W, direction, we came to some*
> *hot springs, which were a great curiosity. . .*

Traveling south in Ruby Valley, along the base of the Ruby Mountains, and finding Harrison Pass, they crossed the mountains and descended on the west side by a small stream that flowed into the South Fork of the Humboldt River:

> *We could see no termination of the valley, nor any*
> *signs of Mary's river, we therefore concluded that*
> *we were too far South, - and passed over the*
> *mountains to the North, where we struck a small*
> *stream running towards the N.W. on this we encamped*
> *and found plenty of grass, - a few fish were caught,*
> *some of which were trout, which led us to the*

> *conclusion that this was a branch of Mary's river.*
> *Distance 18 miles.*

They followed the South Fork of the Humboldt River north and camped in its deep canyon:

> *The creek became perfectly dry and its banks rose to*
> *high perpendicular precipices, so that there was no*
> *other road than the dry bed of the stream. . . we*
> *encamped in a place, affording a little grass and*
> *water - where we could see nothing but the sky.*

Emerging from the South Fork Canyon, they were now on the Humboldt River between Elko and Carlin Canyon. They would now be following the river they had been searching for, but without recognizing it. This is possible because the area where the South Fork meets the main river was probably a large slough. Undoubtedly there were many willows, which would have made it difficult to tell that the stream they had been following had become part of another stream. They traveled down the river six days before being convinced it was the one they were seeking, as Bidwell recorded: "Traveled about 20 miles, course of stream W.N.W. According to the map Mary's river ran W.S.W. Strong doubts were entertained about this being Mary's river. . ." This reference to a map indicates that they had information from someone familiar with the Bonneville party led by Joseph Walker in 1833, and that they were trying to follow his route. Their information could have come from John Marsh, who was encouraging emigrants to come join him in California by sending back letters, directions, and other information. Walker did not go south into Ruby Valley, as this party did, but instead either crossed to the Humboldt River through Secret Pass on the north end of the valley, or went north, without crossing the East Humboldt Mountains, to the headwaters of the Humboldt River at Wells.

The Bidwell-Bartleson party followed the same route as the Walker-Bonneville party through most of Nevada. On reaching the big bend of the river near Winnemucca, they finally realized they were on Mary's River. This is the point where the Little Humboldt River comes in from the north:

> *Having traveled about 5 miles, we all beheld with*
> *delight the course of the river, change to S.W., -*
> *here was excellent grass - it was 3 or 4 feet high,*
> *and stood thick like a meadow, it was a kind of*
> *Bluegrass. . .*

Bartleson was the duly elected captain of the party, but dissension developed among its members. As a result, Bartleson and seven other men left the others in order to travel faster. This separation occurred before the party reached Lovelock and the end of the Humboldt River. Bidwell described Bartleson's departure:

> Capt Bartleson, having got enough meat yesterday to
> last him a day or two, and supposing he would be
> able to reach the mountains of California in 2 or 3
> days, rushed forward with his own mess, consisting
> of 8 persons at a rate entirely too fast for the
> oxen, - leaving the rest to keep up if they could,
> and if they could not it was all the same to him.
> The day was very warm. The Indian Pilot remained
> with us - the river spread into a high, wide swamp,
> covered with high cane grass. . .

After resting near present Lovelock, in an area the later emigrants called the Great Meadows, they crossed the slough that ran from the meadows to form Humboldt Lake. (Walker also crossed this slough at the same place with the Bonneville party.) This writer believes that the emigrants then crossed the West Humboldt Range by Wild Horse Pass, and continued south across the large barren alkali flat that is part of the Carson Sink. They then crossed the sand dunes that extend from Pintail Bay on the east to the "Battle Grounds" on the west, and camped on the West Sloughs in the Carson Sink:

> Crossed Mary's river where it led from the swamp into
> a Lake beyond, - our Pilot led us South on the trail of
> Capt. B - crossed a plain which is covered with water
> the greater part of the year - then came into sand
> hills, among which traveling was very laborious. Saw
> to the W. of us a Lake presenting a sheet of water 20
> or 30 miles in extent. Encamped by another swamp in
> which the water was very nauseous. Distance 28 miles. . .

The lake of twenty or thirty miles extent that Bidwell saw to the west of him was in all probability a mirage which he mistook for water as he looked across the dry alkali flat. The next day's entry in this journal is misleading:

> Crossed Mary's river - it was here running E. leading
> from the lake which we saw to the W. of us yesterday,
> into the swamp by which we staid last night. Our
> course today was S.W. Distance 15 miles - encamped
> upon the Lake.

His Mary's River could have been the Stillwater Slough, but it probably was the New River. This river does not exist now, but at that time it ran east through Fallon about where the present high school is located. The lake on which the party camped was Carson Lake, southeast of Fallon, the location of the Greenhead Hunting Club.

Leaving Carson Lake they traveled in a southwesterly direction to Walker River, striking the river to the west of Weber Reservoir:

> Left the Lake this morning, going into the mountains
> on a S.W. course; today we left the trail of Capt. B.
> and having traveled 19 miles arrived on a stream which
> flowed rapidly, and afforded more water than Mary's
> river. We thought now, without doubt, that we were
> safe on the waters of the St. Joaquin (pronounced St.
> Wawkeen) according to Marsh's letter. Here grew
> willows, balm gilead, and a few cotton woods. The
> course of the stream as far as we could see was S, -
> but we knew not how soon it might take a turn here in
> the Mountains.

They traveled up the river about four miles and crossed at the large bend east of the present town of Wabuska:

> Traveled about 13 miles and only crossed a bend of the
> river, at this place it ran due North, day was hot,
> the creek had dwindled to half its first size.

They followed the West Walker River through Mason Valley and Wilson Canyon into Smith Valley. They continued following the river west through Hoye Canyon and on into Antelope Valley, where they finally faced the Sierra Nevada:

> Advanced up stream about 12 miles and arrived at the
> base of very high mountains, the creek had become a
> small spring branch, and took its rise at no great
> distance in the mountains. But we saw plainly, that
> it was impossible to progress farther without scaling
> the Mts., and our Indian Guides said, they knew no
> further.

Captain Bartleson and his group rejoined the party at this place, having been separated from them for ten days. The reunion was probably in Antelope Valley near the present town of Coleville:

> This morning 4 or 5 men started to ascend several
> of the high peaks, to ascertain if it was possible
> to pass the mountains, just as they were going to

*start Capt. B. came up, he was in rather a hungry
condition, and had been traveling several days
without provisions, excepting a few nuts which they
had purchased from the Indians and which they had
eaten on a very small allowance. . .*

The party now began a search to find a passage over the Sierra Nevada.
Suffering great hardships, they finally crossed near Sonora Pass and emerged
in the San Joaquin Valley in California.

It is believed that the route used by these first emigrants through Nevada,
as here given, is reasonably accurate, although it differs in many respects from
the route given by other writers.

The Bidwell-Bartleson party did not contribute anything new to the trail
used by future emigrants, and no other emigrant party ever followed its route
all the way to California. It has a place in the history of the trail because it
used the so-called "Walker River route" after leaving the Humboldt Sink and
because it was the first emigrant group to travel to California using the central
overland route. The Bidwell-Bartleson party was the "spring branch" - as
emigrants called a small stream - of emigration across Nevada, a branch that
rapidly became a large westward flowing river.

The year after the Bidwell-Bartleson party reached its destination, one
of its members, Joseph Chiles, returned to the states and organized another
group of emigrants. They started for California in 1843, and were the second
group to attempt to take wagons to California by the central route. This party
was known as the Chiles party, or the Chiles-Walker party, since Chiles had the
good fortune to meet mountain man Joseph Walker and persuade him to act as a
guide.

Before the party even reached Nevada their food became dangerously low.
Chiles and a few men on horseback decided to try to skirt the Sierra Nevada on
the north, obtain supplies at Sutter's Fort, and return to the party near present
Lovelock, Nevada. Walker's group was left to its own resources when deep snows
in the Sierra prevented Chiles from returning.

Walker had been to California, and thus knew of a pass in the southern
Sierra. So, with responsibility for women and children, he decided to head south
through Nevada. He went around the east shore of Walker Lake and south by
Bishop, California into Owens Valley. Since the food was gone and the wagons
were now useless, he left them and packed the rest of the way. He had taken

wagons into the present California but not over the Sierra Nevada. By now it was a reality: men, women, and children could go all the way to California, and wagons had been taken most of the way.

The year 1844 saw the start of a well organized party with close family ties; it was known as the Stevens party, or the Murphy-Townsend-Stevens party. This group traveled the Fort Hall, Goose Creek, Humboldt River route as Joseph Walker had done the year before. At the "Great Meadows" near Lovelock, an Indian was destined to change the route of travel. He became known as "Chief Truckee" and he told this party of a river that flowed from the mountains on the west (Truckee River). Over these mountains there were other rivers that flowed to a great valley, where there were many cattle and horses. The leaders knew that he must be talking about Sutter's Fort, now the town of Sacramento. This was a cautious group, so some of the men traveled with Chief Truckee to the present Truckee River to verify the story.

When the Chief's story proved true they decided to try this route. In so doing they established the "Truckee River Route" through the present town of Reno. It was a direct approach to the Sierra Nevada and their ultimate destination, Sutter's Fort.

This was the only emigrant party to follow the Truckee River all the way up to its junction with Donner Creek. They had a very difficult time in the canyon between Verdi, Nevada and the town of Truckee, California. At the junction of the Truckee River and Donner Creek the party divided; some of them followed the river on horseback to its source in Lake Tahoe. This group continued south along the west shore of the lake and probably crossed the mountains by way of McKinney Creek.

Within a few miles of where the party split, those with the wagons came to a lake, which they called Truckee Lake (Donner Lake). It was November and there was snow on the ground, so after examining the mountains to the west of the lake, they decided to attempt to take only five wagons. The rest of the wagons would be left at the lake with three men to guard them for the winter. The five wagons were successfully taken over the summit and most of the way to Sutter's Fort. The following spring the journey was completed, one year from the time it began.

The three men who were left at the lake with the other wagons built a log cabin. This cabin was also used two years later by part of the Donner party when they became trapped in the snows at this same place. The men from the Stevens party soon discovered that there were no wild animals with which to replenish their food supply and that they did not have enough to last the winter. They made snowshoes and started for Sutter's Fort. Traveling on the homemade snowshoes was so cumbersome that one man, an eighteen year old, developed cramps in his legs and could not continue. His friends had to leave him, but he was able to return to the cabin, where he survived alone until the following February. The other two arrived safely at Sutter's Fort and one of them later returned to help his companion over the mountains.

The Murphy-Townsend-Stevens party, in the year 1844, had taken wagons with women and children all the way over the Sierra Nevada and into California. This completed the last segment of the central overland trail up the Truckee River and over Donner Pass. The gate was now open for more emigrants to pour into this foreign land of California. Some enthusiasm was dampened two years later by the tragedy of the Donner party, but even this could not stay the wave of emigration, which was whipped into a fury by the discovery of gold in 1848.

The Bear Flag Revolt and the defeat of the Mexicans made California a part of the United States. Other routes to California were developed, but the most direct was through Nevada and down the valley of the Humboldt River. The journey through Nevada was the worst part of the whole trip for the emigrants and more than half of the distance they traveled in Nevada was in the valley of the Humboldt. The three hundred miles down this valley was indeed a fearful crossing. The emigrants' life along the Humboldt River is of great interest, and an account of the travelers' experiences rightfully precedes any detailed tracing of the trail across Nevada.

"D—N THE HUMBOLDT!"

David Rohrer Leeper

II. Life on the Trail: In the Valley of the Humboldt

The valley of the shadow of death, . . .
Who enters here, leaves hope behind.
William G. Johnston (1849)

It was said that whenever there was a gathering of emigrants on the central overland trail, no matter what the conversation had been it invariably turned to discussion of the Humboldt River, the "Sink" and the "Desert." The Humboldt River was the route the emigrants followed for three hundred monotonous miles; when it ended in the Humboldt Sink they had to make preparations to cross the dreaded Forty Mile Desert.

The emigrants had been on the trail two to three months by the time they reached the Humboldt River. The animals were becoming worn out and the wagons were starting to show the effects of many days travel on the trail. The long, dry, tedious, and dusty pull down this river was bound to take its toll, not only of the wagons and the animals but also of the emigrants.

Thousands of animals died along the Humboldt. How many humans no one knows, but there were many. The torturous trip through this section of Nevada so weakened both animals and humans that many of those who survived the travel down the river succumbed to the Forty Mile Desert that immediately followed. One diarist says he counted 934 graves on this desert, and a relief party reported ministering to the dead and dying.

When the emigrants reached the Humboldt, trouble with the Indians began in earnest. Feed for the animals was a real problem, and starvation for the emigrants themselves was a very real threat. The monotonous travel and anxiety caused some to go insane, and they had to endure days of terrible dust and poor water – or even none at all. The long sought and yet dreaded Humboldt River was the lifeline for thousands crossing this section of the Great Basin; it was the nemesis for hundreds who couldn't hold on and were destined to remain forever on its banks, becoming Nevada's first permanent white residents.

The sadness and problems caused by death on the trail had been witnessed by the emigrants many times before they reached Nevada. It would become almost commonplace before they reached the end of the Humboldt River and the Forty Mile Desert. During the gold rush period there were many families on the trail;

but the majority of emigrants were men traveling in organized companies or just in groups for protection, not knowing each other except by first name. When one of these men died he was buried as an unknown. If he had loved ones waiting to hear from him they would never know his fate. Many husbands, fathers, sons, and other relatives just disappeared into the great unknown of the west:

> *Unfortunately the poor fellow was a stranger to us -*
> *we had met him upon the start & none knew of his name*
> *or the address of his poor mother. The labor &*
> *anxiety of such a journey are so exhausting to the*
> *body & absorbing to the mind that we rarely get even*
> *the name of an associate, much less knowledge of his*
> *history and family.*
>
> Charles D. Ferguson (1850)

> *They were buried in shallow graves, the earth heaped*
> *above them, and a stake bearing the single word*
> *'Unknown' placed at the head.*
>
> John Steele (1850)

Inscribed on one headboard was an epitaph that could apply all along the trail: "whose was he and who were his."

When death came, a grave was dug quickly and the burial completed as soon as possible so the wagons or pack train could move on. Sometimes the wagons were driven over the grave to hide it. It was heartbreaking when a mother had to leave a child in this wilderness and move on. Death took its toll of young and old.

> *About midnight our neighbor approached our campfire*
> *and told us that his only child had just died and he*
> *had come to solicit aid to bury it. We promised that*
> *in the morning his wants should be attended to. We*
> *had an empty cracker box which we made answer for a*
> *coffin, dug a grave in the middle of the road and*
> *deposited the dead child therein. The sun had just*
> *risen and was a spectator to that mother's grief as*
> *she turned slowly but sadly away from that little*
> *grave to persue the long journey before her. We*
> *filled the grave with stones and dirt, and when we*
> *rolled out drove over it. Perhaps we had cheated*
> *the wolf by so doing - perhaps not.*
>
> John Hawkins Clark (1852)

> *Mrs. Barnes died at half past nine. Amandy was taken*
> *sick this morning and died in the afternoon, Mahala*
> *was taken this morning and is not likely to recover.*
> *The three women were sisters.*
>
> John N. Lewis (1852)

*Passed the grave of an emigrant, just buried, the wife
and children still lingering over the new made grave,
the company with which they were traveling having
moved on. A more desolate looking group than that
mother and her five children presented would be hard
to find.*

John Hawkins Clark (1852)

*Coming down this stream we have seen the skulls of a
number of persons who have been buried in '49 - '50 -
'51 and have been dug up by the wolves, and their
bodies left to whiten the plains. And we see a great
many fresh graves of the victims of this year.*

R. H. P. Snodgrass (1852)

Simple grave markers, such as that noted by historian George R. Stewart, also
told the story:

*Mary Jane McClelland
departed this life, Aug. 18th
1849 aged 3 yrs. 4 mos.*

Necessity sometimes made for difficult decisions:

*Found a man dead by the roadside today. Two stakes
were driven into the ground, and over them was drawn
a piece of wagon sheet, under which the man lay. . . .
By his side was a cup of water and a piece of hard
bread. Near by lay a card, with the following on it:
"Please give this man a cup of water and bread if he
needs it. He was not able to travel, and wanted to
be left."*

G. W. Thissell (1849)

When a headboard was used at the grave it was usually some piece off a wagon:

*The board which bears the name "Ralph Holman aged
19 yrs. Drowned Aug. 2, 1850" will soon decay.
Travelers or friend, may unconsciously tread upon
his grave; but there the tears of affection will
never fall.*

John Steele (1850)

Some deaths were due to natural causes, others were caused by murder,
some by suicide, some by drowning, some by accidents, and some by the Indians.
It seems peculiar that there were so many deaths by drowning in this arid section
of the Humboldt Valley. It surely wasn't the swiftness of the water; the
Humboldt was a slow, meandering stream with many sloughs, and it was very
muddy along its sides. The weakened condition of the emigrants and this mud

took their toll.

> We learned there was a man drowned here a few minutes
> before we came up by swiming [sic] the river for grass
> also 4 or 5 other were drowned yesterday and today
> not far from here in the same way.
>> Leander Vaness Loomis (1850)

> Passed the grave of a man found in the river.
>> Eleazer Stillman Ingalls (1851)

> In memory of Samuel Oliver of Waukesha, Wisconsin,
> who was killed by an arrow shot from a party of
> Indians July 5, 1850, while standing guard at night.
>> Lemuel C. McKeeby (1850)

An ode to the Humboldt:

> What mean these graves so fresh and new,
> Along your banks on either side.
> They've all been dug and filled by you,
> Thou guilty wretch, thou homocide.
>
> Now fare thee well, we here shake hands
> And part - I hope - to meet no more -
> I'd rather be in happier hands than
> Longer live upon your shore.
>> Dr. Horace Belknap (1850)

The trials and tribulations on the trail were bound to make for quick tempers. There were many disputes and arguments, and they sometimes resulted in murder:

> From what I can hear, and I speak to almost every
> company I see, I don't think there ever was a body of
> men left the states, on any expedition, that had so
> much quarrelling and fighting, (the strong abusing
> the weak,) as the California expedition of 1849. . . .
> This morn another quarrel in the camp between the
> E[nglishman] and the D - - which resulted in a fight,
> but as neither were very anxious to continue it,
> they were easily seperated.
>> James F. Wilkins (1849)

> Two men of the company had a chunk of a fight one
> got his arm broken & the other his ear nearly bit
> off & otherwise bruised, the weapons used were
> double barrel shot gun clubs teeth & after the
> fight we hitched up & traveled.
>> David DeWolf (1849)

*During an argument, one emigrant, hit another over
the head with a wagon wrench and killed him. A quick
trial followed. A wagon tongue was elevated to make
a gallows pole and the killer was forthwith hanged.*
                                    Richard G. Lillard

*Have news by more packers that just came in that
Capt. Harding of Kentucky had, a few miles back shot
a man who set fire to the grass after leaving camp
& would not allow him to be buried.*
                                    Peter Decker (1849)

Hill where Reed killed Snyder in the Donner party.

The well-known Donner party had its share of murders along the Humboldt and on the desert. Old Hardcoop was left behind on the desert to die. Wolfinger was killed for his possessions. But the best known of all is John Snyder's death by stabbing, following a quarrel between Snyder and James Frazier Reed. This murder has been placed at different locations on the Humboldt River by historians. McGlashen, the original historian of the Donner party, places the murder at Gravelly Ford. Some later writers used McGlashen's location, but it has been proved that it could not have been at Gravelly Ford. One authority places the murder near Stone House, others suggest different locations.

The place of the murder was a fairly difficult sandy ascent near the river where some of the emigrants had to double team.

Trail looking east from the hill where Reed killed Snyder.

These photographs show the location of the murder at Iron Point, and the trail leading to it.

There were many accidents on the trail. Children fell off the wagons and were run over. They received broken bones, other injuries (which were sometimes worse than death when no doctor was available), or were killed outright:

> *Mr. Collins son Geo, about 6 yr. old fell from the*
> *wagon & wheels ran over his head killing him*
> *instantly.*
>
> Arthur M. Menefee (1857)

Accidental discharge of guns accounted for many deaths, and many agonizing injuries subject to frontier surgery:

> *Joseph Londry who ten days ago shot himself through*
> *the left arm the ball went in just above the elbow*
> *on the in side of the arm penetrated under the bone*
> *and through the Mussles cuting off two small vanes*

or arterys comin out just below the joint in the
shoulder. The arm at this time is dead to the elbow
and has been for several days. The flesh had in many
places cleaved from the bone and live varmints had
got in and had got to be half an inch long. The man
felt well at heart tho quite miserble.

I concluded by becoming teased and beged of in every
way to amputate the arm which I this morning done.
Made a good quick operation. My tools consisted of
a basin - jacknife - a small hacksaw - a pair of
pliers or forceps and needle. I amputated the arm
and done it up in very few seconds over one minute.
He stood the operation beyond all calculations and
he did not grone or make the least nois during the
operation . . . I think their is quite a chance for
him to recover.

W. W. Wixom (1851)

The Plains Indians were not a threat to the emigrants in the early days of the migration. On the plains there were so many buffalo that what the emigrants took made little difference to the Indians. In Nevada it was different; the Indians along the Humboldt had very little food and the emigrants' oxen were a temptation they couldn't resist. Nevada Indians also had very few horses, so a stolen one was a real prize.

The Indians in the Humboldt Valley were named Diggers by the emigrants. Owing to the poverty of their environment, they were a poor group. They begged, stole, and killed when they had to; and they contributed to the misery of the journey down this valley. Their favorite trick was to shoot arrows into the cattle while they were grazing at night, so they would have to be left. This meant food for the Indians but hardships for the emigrants:

These (Diggers) are the most degraded people I have
ever seen and certainly the most degraded of the
"Shemitic race of men."

Thomas Cramer (1859)

They were absolutely naked, poor and hungry, and
quite in keeping with the character of the country.
The average stature of these Root Diggers was not
to exceed five feet, and their weight seventy to
ninety pounds. Their faces were pinched and careworn,
while the most abject misery seemed stamped on every
feature, and we looked upon them as types of humanity
in its lowest form.

Reuben Cole Shaw (1849)

> *Scarely a night passed without there making a raid
> upon some camp, and for five hundred miles they were
> excessively troublesome. If they could not drive the
> animals off, they would creep up behind the sage bushes
> in the night and shoot arrows into them, so that the
> animals would have to be left when they would take them
> after the train had passed.*
>
> Alonzo Delano (1849)

> *The Indians are bad along here and have been committing
> all kinds of depredations; on the night of the 4th
> they stole twenty one horses, shot one mule and stripped
> one man naked within one mile of where we are now camped.*
>
> Lemuel C. McKeeby (1850)

> *These Indians will sometimes kill a man for the merist
> trifle of plunder, for a shirt, or even a fish hook.
> They seen not to be aware of any difference, in a moral
> point of view, in the act of killing an antelope, or a
> human being. Stealing, also, is considered as meritorious,
> if they can do it and escape punishment.*
>
> Franklin Langworthy (1850)

The Indians were always blamed for any difficulties, but the trail also had some marauding white men. The latter encouraged the Indian depredations, and sometimes led raids and took part in murders:

> *We now learned of others who had also lost cattle; the
> Indians always got the blame, even though white men
> might be the ringleaders . . . At Stone Point a company
> of emigrants lost some cattle and set out four men to
> search for them. At length they found the cattle, but
> were attacked by the band of robbers, consisting of
> five white men and a number of Indians.*
>
> Tosten K. Stabaek (1852)

Another incident occurred near this same place on the Humboldt River, but further west of the town of Battle Mountain. William Maxwell calls it the "Holloway Massacre," and again, white men were suspected of leading the Indians.

The small Holloway party consisted of Mr. Holloway, his wife and small child, one other woman, and six men. They made a fateful decision and camped too close to the Humboldt River and the bordering willows. Mr. Holloway arose early in the morning to build the fire. Suddenly a shot came from the willows and he fell dead. The others awakened, and as they stood up they, too, were killed by rifle shot and arrows. One man, although wounded, reached the willows and escaped. Mrs. Holloway was in her tent and came out with her baby in her arms to plead for mercy; but then, in fright, she decided to run. She was immediately pierced with shot and arrows and fell face down in the dirt. The Indians came to her, pulled the arrows out, and thrust them again into her body to make certain that she was dead. Mrs. Holloway, although conscious, never moved. The Indians then scalped her and took the baby girl and killed her by dashing her head against a wagon wheel.

A train in the rear came up and pursued the Indians across the river, causing them to drop some of their loot. The rescuing party recovered some of this property and found Mrs. Holloway's scalp. Taking it back, they were surprised to find her still alive. They put her in a wagon and took her to California, where a year later she was seen wearing a headpiece made from her natural hair. She died a short time later, mentally unbalanced.

Sometimes the Indians were punished, either justly or unjustly:

> *This morning we felt like we ought to have satisfaction from the Indians, so we rallied a force of 35 men, by 9 o'clock, who went back and attacked them in their camp and fought them four hours, and thank fortune killed 15 of the rebels.*
>
> John Wood (1850)

> *Some few days since, a train lost some cattle and thirty men started in pursuit. They divided into companies, most of seven each. One company however, had but four men in it. This company came across four Indians and walked up towards them intending to take them prisoners, but when they got within bow shot of the Indians they shot their arrows at them and wounded three of the white men: one in the shoulder, one in the forehead, the other in the wrist. The white men killed three Indians and one ran away. I understand that one Indian wounded all three of the men and had two wounds himself and when he found that the white man would catch him, as he had shot all his arrows, he stopped and told the man to shoot him in the head, which he did. The company found their cattle but they had been killed.*
>
> Israel F. Hale (1849)

The difficulties created by the Indians embittered the emigrants, but a modern writer, putting himself in the shoes of the emigrants, viewed it differently:

*Then we came, maybe 30,000 of us and by popular
opinion, we ought to be greated with bands ready to
be bemedaled, beflowered, and given the keys to every
nook and cranny - For What? For killing all the
game to be found. For catching with willow seines
all the fish. For burning every scrap of fuel to
be found within three miles of the trail. For
exhausting every good well and spring, cutting all
the grass mortal man can carry, leaving a thousand
oxen's bodies to putrefy in the alkaline pools and
ten thousand such carcases in the river and along
the roadside (so thick in places that the route of
the road has had to be altered) creating such a
stench of putridity that hundreds of us have been
made nauseated and several tis said have been
rendered insane.*

> Archer B. Hulbert

The many sloughs and accompanying mud along the circuitous course of
the Humboldt River made it very difficult for the emigrants to get to the water
and grass:

*It is so very crooked in its whole course that I believe
it impossible for one to make a chalk mark as much so.
Frequently I have stood and fished on each side of me
in two different parts of the river, the distance
around being half a mile or more.*

> Vincent Geiger (1849)

*Since reaching this stream, we have been most
wonderfully deceived we had pictured to ourselves,
one of the most grand and beautiful streams which
our country could produce, with beautiful roads
runing along its pleasant banks, and abundants of
the very best of feed, and easy to get, but instead
of that, we find a crooked muddy stream, with a wide
and swampy, bottom so much so that it is utterly
impossible to get horses in to the river at scarcely
any point, the road is obligded to keep out among
the hills, the valley being impassable from the fact
of its being, so muddy.*

> Leander Vaness Loomis (1850)

The crooked river taught some young men a costly lesson:

*We were camped on the Humboldt River, and the morning
was hot and sultry. As the sun rose above the mountain
peaks, the train pulled out of camp. As it started,
six young men . . . put their clothes in the wagon and
took to the water.*

The river was crooked, and the road led from bend to bend in the river. This made many cut-offs. We did not notice that the train was leaving the river, and before we knew it, the wagons were out of sight.

On and on, down the river we went. At times we left the water and ran along on the hot sand and gravel, but soon our fun began to grow serious. The train had taken a cut-off, and left the river. The heat was intense. The sun was almost blistering our backs, which were now as red as lobsters.

It was ten o'clock, and no train could be seen. We left the water and heeled it down the river through the willows, like so many wild men . . . Two o'clock when the train came back to the river and camped, we were still two miles away. . . . Our backs were so blistered we could hardly wear our shirts. At six o'clock we were only twelve hours older, but many years wiser. The train had traveled only twelve miles, while we had traveled many more.

G. W. Thissell (1849)

Meandering Humboldt River.

Besides making it almost impossible to get to the river for grass and water, the sloughs created another problem - mosquitoes:

39

Mosquitoes were as thick as flakes in a snow-storm.
the poor horses whinnied all night, from their
bites, and in the morning the blood was streaming
down their sides.

Margaret A. Frink (1850)

. . . breathed fought bled and died almost with
mosquitoes.

Joseph Curtis Buffum (1847)

Our mules were turned amongst the willows where they
were nearly devoured by the mosquitoes . . . having
spent a restless night amidst swarms of hungary
mosquitoes. To get clear of which I left my blankets
and buttoned around me my India rubber coat, and
strolled around through the sage for some time to
get clear of the hungary myriads, but I had not lain
down more than two minutes before I was literally
covered.

Madison B. Moorman (1850)

The emigrants had been on the trail three or four months, and some longer, before they reached the end of the Humboldt River. Their food supply was becoming low, and in many cases it was completely gone:

Tonight we eat the last of our provisions. We are
not alone in our trouble in this respect; there are
thousands that have been running out of grub for
the past week.

Lemuel C. McKeeby (1850)

Pushing all we can on account of scarcity of
provisions, every wagon of us not having laid in
a sufficient quantity, chiefly on account of
false reports, from almost everyone, of the
distance. We have traveled about as far already
as we understood would take us to the mines, and
have, as yet, full five hundred miles to go.

Dr. J. S. Shepherd (1850)

Here on the Humboldt, famine sits enthroned, and
waves his scepter over a dominion expressly made
for him.

Horace Greeley (1859)

Hunger sometimes prevailed over pride or a weak stomach:

I have noticed several dead horses, mules, and oxen,
by the roadside, that had their hams cut out to eat
by the starving wretches along the road, but for my
own part, I will eat the lizzards which infest the

*sage bushes, before I will eat the stock that died
from the alkali . . . Often, almost daily, some
poor starved fellow comes up to the wagon and pray
us in God's name to give or sell him a crust of
bread, some of them asserting that they have eaten
no food for two or even three days.*

Eleazer Stillman Ingalls (1850)

*I have seen a man eating his lunch, and gravely sitting
on the carcass of a dead horse, and we frequently take
our meals amidst the effluvia of a hundred putrescent
carcasses.*

Franklin Langworthy (1850)

*Here are, in this camp, many cases of suffering,
having had no bread for weeks, and they have become
tired of asking, and hundreds are living on half
rations . . . This morning we eat the last pound
of beef, which had some few maggots in it, but I
must acknowledge that it tasted well.*

John Wood (1850)

A new source of food was found by some of the hungry travelers:

*We came on the bank of the river and all go to
catching what we term ground rats; they are little
mouse colored animals that live in the ground, not
quite as large as a small rat, long in body, and
having a flat tail, but not bushy like the squirrel.
We caught enough of these little animals to make a
good meal for our supper and had some left over for
breakfast.*

Lemuel C. McKeeby (1850)

The oxen, mules, and horses suffered even more than the emigrants.
Grass was very scarce except on the headwaters of the river:

*The stream itself does not deserve the name of river
being only a good sized creek . . . For the first
days travel in its valley the grass is splendid,
then the valley begins to narrow and feed to get
poorer & less of it all the rest of its course, till
for the last 80 miles, except in special spots we
could hardly get enough for our mules to eat &
water barely drinkable from saline & sulphurous
impregnation & having a milky color. I think Baron
Humboldt would feel but little honored by his name
being affixed to a stream of so little pretension.*

Elisha D. Perkins (1849)

41

Already the grass is so scarce that we will not be enabled to get through, if at all, by merely the skin of our teeth, & what the seven thousand teams behind us are to do - God Almighty only knows.
                    Vincent Geiger (1849)

Our stock almost giving out. We have now traveled three days with little or no feed. Our stock looks badly.
                    George Willis Read (1850)

Our cattle are now getting so poor that it takes two to make a shadow.
                    John Wood (1850)

Our case had been a hard one for the last 250 miles. All along the road for that distance is lined with the carcasses of dead horses and cattle; the stench from them as we pass is horrid and sickening.
                    Lemuel C. McKeeby (1850)

There is more property from the head of the Humboldt to Salmon Trout such as horses, mules, cattle, and wagons, goods, etc. than there will be money taken by the same men from California in one year and there is not the one half that there will be.
                    Thomas Christy (1850)

Kit Carson says that the Humboldt is the burying ground for horses and oxen. We pass daily great numbers of dead stock, at the camping grounds, in the sloughs, and in the river; the river is nothing but horse broth seasoned with alkali and salt.
                    Eleazer Stillman Ingalls (1850)

The cure for the poor cattle certainly did not help their fate:

A cure for the alkalied cattle was a plug of tobacco between two slices of bacon. This cured cattle or killed them. Another remedy was to feed them acid and bleed them.
                    Richard G. Lillard

The prescribed cure for "hollow horn" was just as bad:

Some have hollow horn; for that we bore the horn and put in salt, pepper and water until it runs out of their noses. They have another disease called hollow tail; for that they split the tail where it is hollow.
                    Israel F. Hale (1849)

Today we travel along the Humboldt Valley at sixty miles an hour with

42

little thought that the emigrants spent four to five days traveling the distance that we can go in one hour. Even at this speed some of these long stretches seem never ending to us. Just think how it must have been traveling at the slow pace of an oxen.

Some of the weary travelers described the monotony of the Humboldt Valley by stating that the scenery did not seem to change. The mountains ahead seemed as far away at the end of the day as they did in the morning:

> We have traveled so long among the mountains, and all bearing the same general appearance, that we seemed to be stationary instead of changing our position every day. In looking around me I seem to be in a deep blue ocean of air, with the distance mountains around as the shore.
> C. W. Smith (1850)

> The monotony of each days march seems to increase with the desolation which more and more abounds.
> William Johnston (1849)

> Our trip down the Humboldt has been the hardest portion of the road so far but we are pretty near through with it. There is such a sameness about it I thought I would omit giving the proceedings of each day.
> Richard O. Hickman (1852)

There was not even a tree to break the monotony:

> On the whole length of this River, we have not seen a tree or stick of wood.
> William H. Kilgore (1850)

> The Humboldt has no timber at all except willow bushes. I did not see a tree along its whole course.
> Lorenzo Sawyer (1850)

> I have not seen a tree or shrub, except bunch willows, for almost 300 miles, and they tell me we will find none until we reach the Carson river, 100 miles ahead.
> John Wood (1850)

Many of the emigrants had guide books such as the Mormon Guide, Ware's, or others; but much of the information in these guides, as well as that received from other sources, was misleading:

July 20, 1849 came to the river and nooned - grass
only tolerable. We begin to be greatly disappointed
in our calculations of finding good grass on this
measly Humboldt as Mr. Ware had prepared us to expect.
Let no traveler hereafter be governed by Wares Guide
as it is perfectly worthless.
                              Bennett C. Clark (1849)

Fremont had not traveled on the Humboldt River and wrote misleading information
from hearsay:

I would ask the learned & descriptive Mr. Fremont
and the elegant & imaginative Mr. Bryant, where was
the beautiful valley, the surpassing lovely valley
of Humboldt? Where was the country presenting the
most splendid "agriculture features?" Where the
splendid grazing, the cottonwoods lining the banks
of their beautiful meandering stream, & every thing
presenting the most interesting & picturesque
appearance of any place they ever saw?
                              Vincent Geiger (1849)

Sometimes the monotony of the Humboldt valley was broken by thunder and
lightning storms; such as this woman experienced under difficult circumstances:

Rain! Rain! Rain! During all P.M. yesterday the
black clouds in the W. & low distant thunder betokened
showers ahead. After encamping (which we did not do
until sun set & after) we got a very hasty supper &
at about 9 commenced and continued for over 2 hours
one of the most terrific thunder showers I have ever
witnessed. The rain came down in torrents, - floods -
the thunder fair shook the earth, and the wind blew
little short of a hurricane - the whole lighted up almost
every instant by the deep red glare of the burning
lightening. Albert had been complaining during the day
of head ache & other pains. Come into camp very sick
and during this terrible storm we were in our wagon
with a lighted lantern, curtains tightly fastened,
and some of the rain (very little) driveing through
our hitherto water proof cover; he writhing with pains
in the head, back and bones, almost screaming with
agony under a burning fever & a hard pulse - in short
a very critical case of some acute fever, requiring the
best care of a skillful physician & the comforts of
civilized life - but instead of that he had neither
but was cooped up in a 3½ x 9 box - dependant only
upon me for medical aid - & I without the skill of a
doctor and with a very small variety of medicines was

forced to 'take the responsibility.' First got down
cathartic - pains increasing gave during the night
repeated small doses morphine - in morning an emitic -
today pains gone & much better but no appetite & much
nausea.

Addison Moses Crane (1852)

All of these troubles made the emigrants' travel down the Humboldt River a gruesome journey, but worst of all were the water and dust:

Today our road lay along the river most of the time,
occasionally leaving it for a few miles. Dust!
Dust!! Dust!!!

David Jackson Staples (1849)

The road along this river, is so dusty, that it makes
travelling very disagreeable. As a general thing the
dust along the river is from 6 to 8 inches deep, being
of the very lightest kind, so that the least wind will
stir it up, and almost blind a person. I have seen it
so thick that we could not see wagons that were not
more than 4 or 5 rods ahead.

Leander Vaness Loomis (1850)

The Dust! no person can have the least idea, by a
written description - it certainly is intolerable - but
that does not half express my meaning - we eat it, drink
it, breath it, night and day, the atmosphere being loaded
with it. It effects people's eyes - but everybody had
horribly sore lips - in fact, that is the greatest bane
of the route.

Dr. J. S. Shepherd (1850)

All felt a real satisfaction and no little gratitude in
bidding adieu to the Great Humboldt Valley with its
weeks of clouds of gray, alkaline dust encompassing us
until it was often difficult to distinguish one another.
It had permeated everything we possessed - our covered
wagon, animals, food, clothes, faces, ears, eyes, throat -
and left burning, itching, bleeding chapped conditions
of the skin from which we suffered much distress both
night and day.

Charles F. True (1859)

And now we begin to suffer in earnest. Our lips bleed
almost everytime we speak, and our mouths and throats
are sore from the effects of the dust, heat and bad
water . . . The water in the valley is growing worse.

R. H. P. Snodgrass (1852)

During the first days on the upper part of the river, the water was generally

45

good; but it became progressively worse as the travelers descended the river:

> We have a river to draw from but such water - warm as
> fresh milk and impregnated with alkali and a taste of
> salt to such a degree that we cannot use it until
> after the poison is killed by heating. We boil all
> the water we drink, and then it is barely fit for use.
> Sometimes we find a spring near the river edge and
> among the tall wild grass, and if it is full of snakes,
> frogs, and other reptiles, it is all right. We drive
> them out, and take a drink ourselves; but if the water
> looks black, and we can find no water varmint, not
> even a snake, we let it alone.
>
> John Hawkins Clark (1852)

> The water of the river is not good at best, but at this
> time is unwholesome from the great number of dead
> animals lying in it. You will sometimes see 20 and 30
> dead animals in 2 or 3 miles.
>
> George Willis Read (1850)

> For about ten days the only water we had was obtained
> from the pools by which we would camp. These pools
> were stagnant and their edges invariably lined with
> dead cattle that had died while trying to get a drink.
> Selecting a carcass that was solid enough to hold us
> up, we would walk into the pool on it, taking a blanket
> with us, which we would swash around and get as full of
> water as it would hold, then carry it ashore, two men,
> one holding each end, would twist the filthy water out
> into a pan, which in turn would be emptied into our
> canteens, to last until the next camping place. As the
> stomach would not retain this water for even a moment,
> it was only used to moisten the tongue and throat.
>
> Gilbert L. Cole (1852)

Even in adversity some of the emigrants had a sense of humor about the awful water:

> The river water which we have to use is detestable; it
> is fairly black and thick with mud and filth; but there
> is one advantage one has in using it - it helps to
> thicken the soup which would be rather thin without it.
>
> Henry Sterling Bloom (1850)

As bad as the water was, however, these emigrants were better off than those coming down the river in dry years:

> We crossed Mary's River which at this season was entirely
> dry, and water was to be had only in deep pools.
>
> Nicholas Carriger (1846)

46

Humboldt River in a dry year. This picture was taken between Golconda and Battle Mountain in 1977.

Rolled down stream today 13 miles, the river generally dry.
                                    Virgil Pringle (1846)

The river here is nothing more than a mud ditch winding through the alluvial deposit of the valley in the most crooked course that could be marked out for it.
                                    William Swain (1849)

There has been but little running water in the channel of the river for two or three days travel but below our last encampment a creek comes in from the north and there is now plenty of water.
                                    James Mathers (1846)

The creek that came from the north was the Little Humboldt River near Winnemucca. Generally the stretch from Winnemucca down was the driest and worst part of the trip.

Twenty years before this horde of emigrants descended on the Humboldt

River, Peter Skene Ogden, the man who discovered the river, gave a good description of what it looked like. Ogden was trapping beaver for the Hudson Bay Company when he wrote the following in his diary, in 1829:

> The water in this river is very muddy, warm and in my opinion very unwholesome, for in all my travels in the Snake Country the camp have never been so sickly as in this stream. Add to this from its source to its discharge in Unknown Lake on both sides is one continued swamp covered with frogs, toads and garter snakes and this also I presume does not tend to render the water good and to render the assortment of reptiles complete. Rattlesnakes alone are wanting, if any, they are very scarce, not one have I seen.
>
> As regards animals although the hunters have for the last three days hunting on the mountains, only two antelope have they killed and report having seen eight as this is the season that animals resort to the rivers and as we have not seen one on its banks I may consequently conclude they are very scarce, and woe to them who depend to them for support - in wild fowl, although the country is well adapted for them, not over numerous. Pelicans are however the reverse, particularly in the lower part of the river & they have noble sport pasturing on frogs & toads. As for birds they are numerous and amongst the number - Whip-poor-will, the first I have seen on west side of the mountains, how the latter has found his way to this distance quarter I leave for others to determine.
>
> In fur animals our traps have given a convincing proof that there are beaver, having including fall hunt, given us fourteen hundred. Other scarcely any. Muskrats although the country favourable for them not numerous. Minks scarcely any . . .
>
> The length of this river may be computed at 120 miles that we have seen of it and from its source 135 miles; its breadth may average twenty yards and contains to a large swamp seen on the 27th ultimo a large body of water. Then it becomes a dimunitive stream losing half its size and water, nearly bare of willows and from the report of Indians finishes its course in the lake, and this ends my remarks on the Unknown River and although I have given it the latter name Swampy River would be more applicable to it if a stranger should seek it. By the trappers it is known as Pauls River as he must remain on it until the Great Trumpet shall sound.

Today we think of the Humboldt River as just an old stream, slowly and serenely winding its way down the valley it created; but the emigrants could find only harsh words to describe it, never a word of praise. Yet what would they have done without the Humboldt River? As bad as the water was, it was better than nothing, and it was necessary. Without this river the thousands of emigrants could not have crossed this barren section of the trail. No practical trail existed to the north of Nevada, and the trails to the south could not have been traveled successfully by so many people. The Humboldt wasn't a pleasant swift-running stream with cool waters dashing over the rocks like the Truckee River; but it was in the right place, and it was the guide that thousands followed successfully.

Maybe it deserved to be called the "Humbug River" or the "Hellboldt River," to have its name changed many times from the Unknown River to Swampy River - Ogden's River - Paul's River - Barren River - St. Mary's River - Muddy River - Mary's River and finally the Humboldt:

> *We have seen more suffering and passed through more hardships since we struck what has been called the beautiful humboldt, than in all the rest of our journey.*
>
> Leander Vaness Loomis (1850)

Yet, for all its hardships, the Humboldt did have one redeeming feature. The obstacles it created for the emigrants easily erased from their minds the many hardships they had encountered before reaching its banks.

The emigrants traveling through the valley of the Humboldt were a cosmopolitan group composed of many nationalities, with Germans and Irish predominant. There were doctors, ministers, lawyers, politicians, blacksmiths, storekeepers, farmers, laborers, and people from all walks of life. Some were black, some were poor and others rich. Some were thieves, bank robbers, or murderers running away from the law, others were respectable law abiding people. Many were religious and were seeking a better place to practice their faith. Some were leaving the cholera-filled valleys of the Mississippi and the Missouri to seek health in a new land. Others were adventurous and were going to satisfy their curiosity. A new country meant an opportunity to start over for those who had failed or a chance for the others to better themselves. Some had sold everything they owned to raise money to furnish the necessary outfit, others were being "grub staked," as we call it. A backer furnished their outfit in return for as much as half of the gold they found for a period of two years.

49

In the years 1849 and 1850, gold was the big attraction.

The trail produced both sadness and joy, and certainly it produced peculiarities:

> *At this place we saw a singular vehicle drawn by two
> horses. It belonged to a man from Milwaukee, who, in
> company with two men, were traveling with it to
> California. It was a cart, having tires a foot wide,
> and two sets of spokes to each wheel. The bed was an
> immense tin box, made water-tight, having a framework
> upon the inside, to strengthen it. The owner was
> forming a guide book for the use of future travelors,
> and within the huge tin box, was a roadometer of an
> ingenious construction. When they started, the carriage
> had six wheels, all of the same construction, and was
> drawn by six horses, besides which there was a curious
> piece of machinery fixed within the bed for the purpose
> of propelling this strange locomotive by hand, in case
> the horses should fail . . . At this time, he had lost
> four of his horses, and had cut down the ponderous
> chariot to a cart for two horses. He had expended near
> two thousand dollars to get started in this way, and
> now seemed to be in somewhat reduced circumstances . . .
> His horses were now low in flesh, and his cart quite
> too heavy a load for them to draw.*
>
> Franklin Langworthy (1850)

Two partners had a quarrel. One owned the oxen and the other the wagon; so they cut the wagon in two, made carts, divided the oxen, and each went his way. Two other men traveled with a hand cart calculated to carry 200 pounds. One man pulled and the other pushed. One boy came all the way with just a cow for a pack animal, while another man went down the Humboldt with a wheelbarrow. Mrs. Ponds walked 1500 miles from the Missouri River to Ragtown so her eight children could ride.

There was also Lucinda, who had her eyes on the men and was married and divorced, so to speak, several times along the trail. Maybe we should call her a "wagon-mate." One man's wife, who kept the train in a turmoil to the Carson River, took a fancy to a trader she met there. Her husband sold her to him for three hundred dollars, a move that met with general approval: "It was a day of rejoicing when we saw her leave the train. The trader took her to Hangtown and gave her to a gambler, and that was the last we heard of her."

In 1849, a newspaper article announced that:

*Mr. Rufus Porter had practically completed his Aerial
Steamboat - when completed would be able to carry
passengers to California for $100.00 including board
and return passage - to go to California in 2 days,
if the winds were favorable and 5 otherwise.*

It is hard to believe that a man drove 2,000 turkeys from Independence to
California or that another man trained a horse to point like a dog, with his head
out and tail straight. And maybe the house cat, Jip, did save a little girl from
starvation on the Humboldt:

*For the next two weeks, while traveling down the Humboldt,
almost every morning there was a rabbit at the tent door.
All knew that the faithful house cat, Jip, had brought
them there . . . none can make Phillip Philly believe
but that Jip saved his sister Mary's life.*
                    G. W. Thissell (1849)

On one occasion a death, a funeral, a wedding, and a birth occurred within two
hours time and a space of two miles diameter, along the trail.

The overland trail in Nevada led through a barren land that defied anyone
to cross it; its beauty was to be discovered by later inhabitants, not by the
emigrants. One fourth of the whole journey these people made was in Nevada --
500 of the 2,000 miles from the Missouri River to Sutter's Fort. To them, Nevada
was a necessary evil that had to be conquered, and conquered it was by groups
who were well organized and led by experienced people. The gold fever also
drew onto the trail people who were unprepared for the ordeal; they were not
experienced with handling animals and knew nothing of survival from the land.
Crossing Nevada was difficult for the best prepared emigrants and almost
impossible for those not prepared, yet thousands did cross successfully. Some
of these emigrants returned later to make Nevada their home. They transformed
part of this barren land into a more hospitable place.

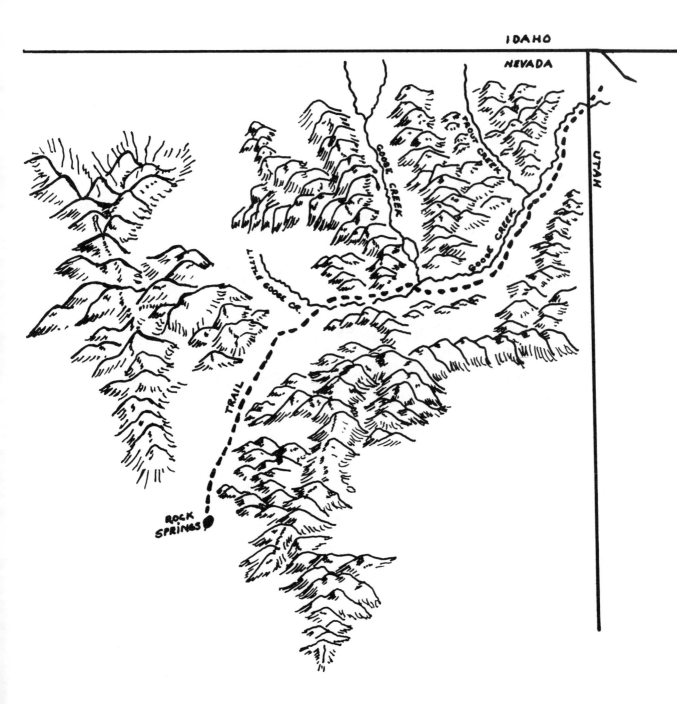

This is the beginning of the emigrants five hundred mile journey across Nevada.

III. Starting Out: Approaches to the Humboldt and on to Elko

The central overland trail to California came into Nevada in the northeast corner of Elko County. The emigrants entered on a stream they called Goose Creek, which still bears that name:

> *This morning got an early start and moved up Goose*
> *Creek about 14 miles, roads good.*
>
> Leander Vaness Loomis (1850)

Goose Creek Valley. Depression in center of picture
made by emigrants' wagons.

The trail followed up Goose Creek to its junction with Little Goose Creek, and then up Little Goose Creek through a rough and rocky canyon:

> *Struck camp and traveled up Goose Creek 8 miles here*
> *the Creek forks the main branch turning to the right*
> *we followed up the left branch 4 miles through a canyon*
> *with high rocky bluffs on both sides the road being*
> *rough & rocky.*
>
> David DeWolf (1849)

Emigrant trail along Goose Creek.

Junction of Goose Creek and Little Goose Creek. Here the
emigrants left Goose Creek and followed to the left on Little Goose Creek.

We traveled one mile farther up Goose Creek and left
it to the right, passed up a branch of it four miles
through a very crooked canon of a great many small
rocks.

Cyrus C. Loveland (1850)

Little Goose Creek Canyon.
The canyon is full of small volcanic rocks
that caused the emigrants a lot of trouble.

Before leaving Goose Creek some of the emigrants put their names on "Record Rock." Some left their names as an idle gesture, but they also provided information for friends and relatives who followed behind. One hundred and thirty years later it gives one a thrill to see these names, inscribed by people heading toward the end of their rainbow – the gold fields of California:

This morn the first object which we passed was Record
Rock, upon right of our way. It is a huge sandstone
bluff in which the action of winds and rain have worn
large cavities and where thousands have, 'For fame's
neglect to atone,' inscribed their names there, perchance
thinking it might, at some future day, afford to some
dear friends who should be winding their weary way through

55

*this lone wilderness a momentary pleasure in knowing
that they were standing just where that dear one had
stood, years before, and gazed with the same feeling
of delight with which we now look upon it.*
Harriet S. Ward (1853)

Record Rock.
The emigrants carved their names in these cavities
and on the soft surface on the outside.

*We passed a singular rock composed of sand stone the
outside being hard & inside quite soft, so soft one
can cut it with a knife it was singular shaped with
large cavities in it & in the different cavities were
a large number of names.*
David DeWolf (1849)

*Passed Record Bluff which is a sandstone, upon which
is written the names of many travelers who camped on
Goose Creek having traveled 15 miles.*
Velina A. Williams (1853)

Emigrant names on Record Rock.

Emigrant names on Record Rock.

After leaving Goose Creek and its tributary, the trail entered a more arid country. Poor grass, abandoned wagons, dead stock, and graves became more common - a forewarning of what was yet to come:

> *The valley in which we are traveling is nearly level, having upon the right and left hand a stupendous amphitheater of naked, barren mountains. Numerous graves of emigrants are here scattered along by the wayside, and the effluvia of dead animals fills the surrounding atmosphere.*
>
> Franklin Langworthy (1850)

> *Wrecked wagons are becoming a matters of almost too frequent occurrence to attract observation.*
>
> William G. Johnston (1849)

> *We followed up Goose Creek and a tributary for about ten miles, when we struck out across a high, dry country destitute of vegetation, except wild sage. After going twelve miles, we came to Thousand Spring Valley.*
>
> C. W. Smith (1850)

Rock Spring.

Rock Springs to Thousand Springs Valley

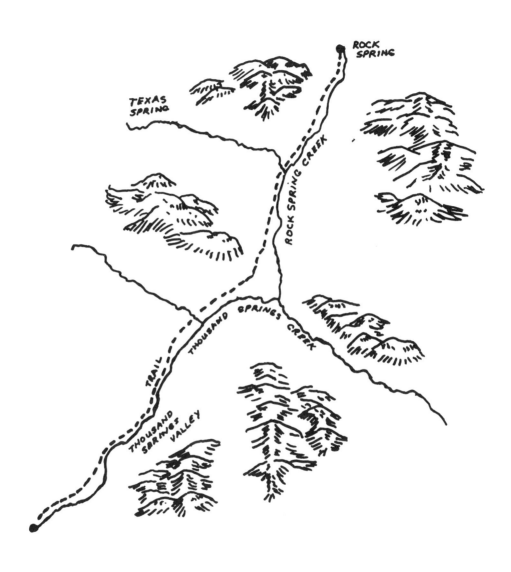

This section of the trail approaches Highway 93 from the northeast.
Water and feed for the animals would not yet become a problem but fatigue on
both man and animals would begin to show.

Before entering Thousand Spring Valley some of the emigrants found a supply of good water at Rock Spring:

Twelve miles farther brought us to Rock Spring this spring comes out of the bottom or under a large rock.
W. W. Wixom (1851)

On entering this valley, a little to the right, under a ledge of rocks, is a spring of good clear water, though a little warm when first taken out, it is called 'Rock Springs.'
P. L. Platt (1849-1850)

Emigrant trail approaching Thousand Spring Valley.

Thousand Spring Valley was a main camping place. Here the emigrants encountered a great wonder, boiling hot springs within a few feet of a spring of cold water:

Passed down the valley over some few hills, passing several of the finest springs we have ever seen. This is called Thousand Spring Valley.
David Jackson Staples (1849)

Here we come up with a string of teams that reach down the valley as far as we could see.
                    Lemuel C. McKeeby (1850)

Thousand Spring Valley.

We passed a number of hot springs early this morning, they were hot enough to boil an egg in a short time within 50 yards of them was another spring of water as cold as ice.
                    Elizabeth Page (1849)

There is very good drinking water within about three feet of the hottest so you can with one hand dip up hot water and the other cold at the same time.
                    Cyrus C. Loveland (1850)

The trail then led in a westerly direction out of Thousand Spring Valley toward Highway 93, which runs between Wells and Jackpot.

The trail branched, the right branch heading into Bishop Creek Canyon and following the creek through it. The emigrants called this creek "Kanyon Creek" and this section of the trail the Mormon Trace:

61

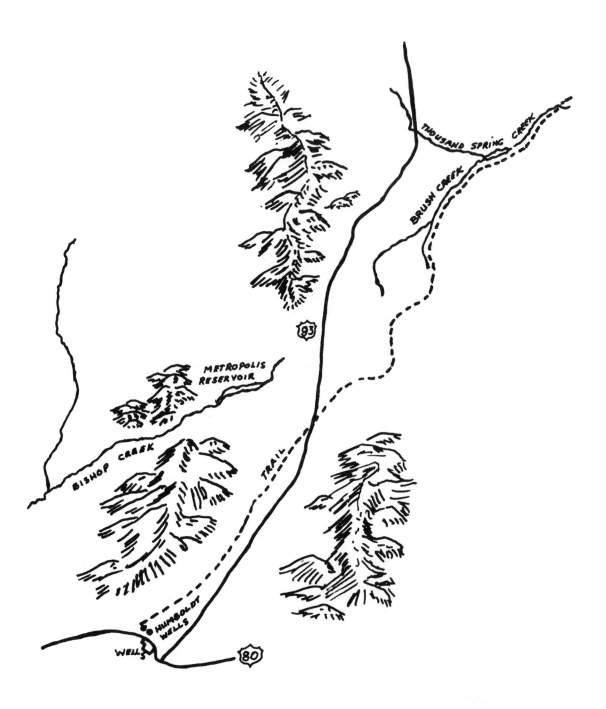

This section ends on the northern outskirts of the town of Wells. Here is a small marsh with some springs which were called wells. This is considered the beginning of the Humboldt River.

*We made down the right hand road two miles and
camped . . . traveled three miles came to a small
stream running between the mountain the water
clear and cold it is called Kanyon Creek we crossed
it nine times . . . the road very rough and rocky
for four or five miles about half way through the
gorge is a warm spring in which we had the finest
bath.*

W. W. Wixom (1851)

The emigrants who took the left branch headed in a southwesterly direction
toward the present town of Wells, where there were some springs, now called
"Humboldt Wells." This is considered by many people as the place where the
Humboldt River begins:

*We left the Morman Trace which leads over to Kanyon
Creek, and passed through a valley to a branch of
the Humboldt River. At this point where we left
the Morman Trace, we found an excellent spring of
pure cold water, as cold as ice water.*

Eleazer Stillman Ingalls (1850)

HUMBOLDT WELLS

THESE SPRINGS, SEEN AS MARSHY SPOTS AND SMALL PONDS OF WATER IN
THE MEADOWS HERE, ARE THE HUMBOLDT WELLS. A HISTORIC OASIS ON
THE CALIFORNIA EMIGRANT TRAIL. HERE DURING THE PERIOD 1845 – 1870
HUNDREDS OF COVERED WAGONS EACH YEAR RESTED AND REFITTED FROM
THEIR ARDUOUS JOURNEY UP RAFT RIVER, PAST THE CITY OF ROCKS,
ACROSS THE GOOSE CREEK RANGE AND DOWN THOUSAND SPRINGS VALLEY,
AND PREPARED FOR THE GRUELING 300 MILE TREK ALONG THE HUMBOLDT
VALLEY. RUTS OF THE OLD EMIGRANT TRAIL WINDING DOWN TO THE SPRINGS
MAY YET BE SEEN ON THE SLOPES ABOVE THEM AND TO THE NORTHWEST.

THE CITY OF WELLS, FIRST ESTABLISHED AS THE WATER STOP OF HUMBOLDT
WELLS ON THE CENTRAL PACIFIC RAILROAD IN SEPTEMBER 1869, IS NAMED
FROM THESE SPRINGS. ITS NAME WAS SHORTENED TO WELLS IN 1873.

STATE HISTORIC MARKER NO. 45
NEVADA STATE PARK SYSTEM
AND
NORTHEASTERN NEVADA HISTORICAL SOCIETY

Historical marker near the town of Wells, Nevada.

Here we descended into a valley. Five miles brought
us to several deep holes in a wet marshy valley to
the left of the road filled with water.
Lorenzo Sawyer (1850)

Humboldt Wells.
Many people consider this the beginning of the Humboldt River.

After leaving the Humboldt Wells, or emerging from Bishop Creek Canyon to the
north, the emigrants would travel separate trails for a few more miles before
coming together again.

Now they began to feel that they were either on or near the much discussed
Humboldt River. The old trapper Broken Hand Fitzpatrick had advised, "find
the Humboldt River and follow it to its end and then west ever west." This is
what most of the travelers did:

> *About noon we reached the headwaters of Humboldt, or*
> *Mary's River, the latter being the name by which it*
> *is commonly known to trappers and mountaineers. Its*
> *length is about three hundred miles, and our route*
> *follows it the entire distance. Where we struck it,*

it was scarcely more than a rivulet, and almost hidden
from sight by the tall grass bent over it.
William G. Johnston (1849)

The valley about the head waters of Mary's river is a
most beautiful valley. You will see the Humboldt
mountains not far distance on your left, covered
with everlasting snows.
P. L. Platt (1849-1850)

We came to Mary's River, or Humboldt, as some call
it, today. All the emigrants dread this river, but
we found some grass, which is more than we expected,
as Mr. Sawyer says there was very little here when
he came up in '49.
Lorenzo Sawyer (1850)

From the headwaters, the emigrants began their journey down the river toward the present town of Elko. In the high water years they had to make many detours on this section, but generally they had good grass and water. They did not have the difficulties they were to encounter farther down the river. They traveled on both sides of the Humboldt, and the trail changed from one year to the next depending on the amount of water in the river. The year 1849 was a dry year, so the trail stayed close to the river and went through the canyons:

The bottom is much cut up with slues which in a time
of high water are filled with water preventing emigrants
from reaching grass without considerable trouble. At
this time the river is very low and most of the slues
are dry or impassable.
D. B. Andrews (1852)

1850 was a wet year with high water, and the many sloughs were full and very muddy. That year the trail was away from the river and the emigrants had to make long detours around the canyons:

Willows along the river banks supplied us with fuel,
and it was our sole dependence for water which had
to be carried for long distances, occasioning great
labor, for our camps were remote from the stream.
William G. Johnston (1849)

At night we reached the Humboldt again after having
been from it some thirty five miles. This portion
of the road is new. The usual road is near the
river, but could not be traveled now on account of
high water.
C. W. Smith (1850)

The various creeks combine on this section to form a sizable stream. The emigrants now knew that they were on the long sought and yet feared Humboldt River.

*The road last year followed down the bottoms, but
this year the water is so high, that the bottoms are
one complete swamp, and as a consequence we have to
keep on the sage plains and cross ridges, making the
road longer and worse to travel and also to wade in
the mud and cut grass for our stock.*

Eleazer Stillman Ingalls (1850)

Near Elko, one traveler returning to the states observed the hot springs:

*A few miles below our camp on the south side of the
river as [is] a singular lot of hot springs which
boil and bubble like cauldron[s] and send off a large
quantity of hot water into the river which is only
a few rods from the springs.*

James Clyman (1846)

The hot springs near Elko, Nevada.

A short distance west of these springs, travelers on the main Humboldt River
route were joined by other emigrants who had entered Nevada by another trail,
the Hastings Cutoff.

67

Halleck to the South Fork of the Humboldt River

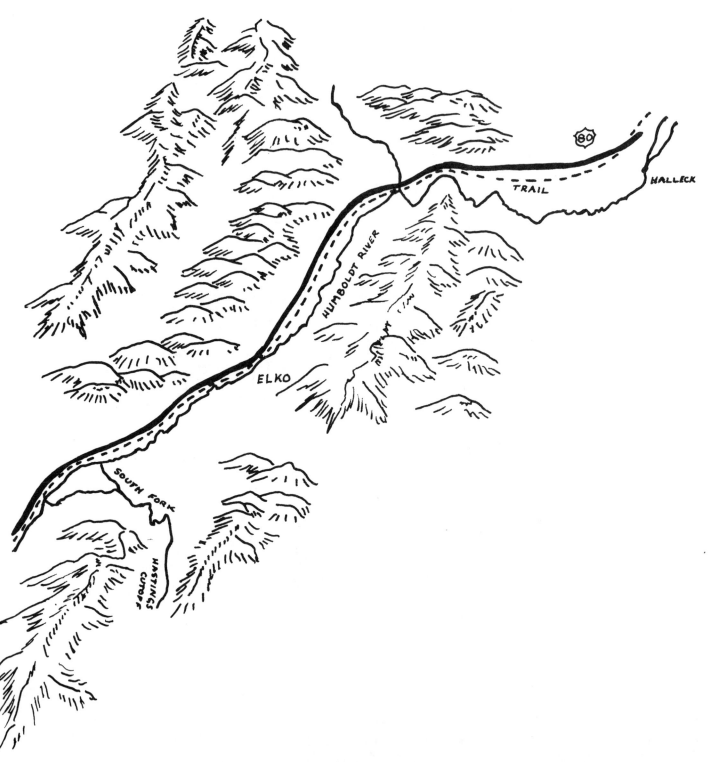

The emigrants had to make a few detours away from the river on this part of the trail but there were not any difficult obstacles to overcome.

IV. The Hastings Cutoff

After crossing the Rocky Mountains, some emigrants chose to leave the established trail, which went on to Fort Hall, Goose Creek, and the Humboldt River. Instead they took a new trail into Salt Lake Valley and across the Great Salt Desert. Those taking this latter route entered Nevada at Pilot Peak, southeast of the town of Wells and north of Wendover, on the Nevada-Utah line. Once in Nevada, the trail proceeded through Ruby Valley, over the Ruby Mountains, and then northward along Huntington Creek and the South Fork of the Humboldt River, leaving that stream shortly before it joined the main Humboldt River west of Elko.

This route was called the Hastings Cutoff. It was established in 1846 by Landsford Hastings, a young, ambitious, well-educated man who had dreams of becoming an important person in California. It is best remembered as the route taken by the ill-fated Donner party of 1846.

The Donner party was formed west of the Rocky Mountains when a number of emigrants decided to take the Hastings Cutoff. Before this, two Donner families had been parts of other groups such as Colonel Russell's or Governor Boggs'. When the Donner party was organized it included just over seventy people and was composed of many families; those of the two Donner brothers, the Reeds, the Breens, the Kesebergs, the Murphys, the Wolfingers, the McCutchens, other families and some single men. Later additions between Fort Bridger and the Wasatch Mountains increased the total number in the party to eighty-seven.

Lansford Hastings is blamed for the tragedy of the Donner group. There is no doubt that he was negligent in not being more certain of his route, and in leading men, women, and children along a trail he himself had previously taken only part way – and that on horseback. In 1845, Hastings returned to California from the east. It is said that he intended to go to Oregon and lead a group from there to California. Why then did he change his mind and decide to guide emigrants on a new route that he had never traveled in its entirety?

When Hastings arrived at Sutter's Fort in December of 1845, John C. Fremont was there. Fremont had made his exploration of 1845 around the Great Salt Lake and then to the west, "discovering a new route." He entered Nevada on its eastern boundary the same as Hastings was to do the following year, and traveled into the Ruby Valley and across the Ruby Mountains. Hastings and Fremont discussed this route that winter at Sutter's Fort and it is reasonable to assume that Hastings was convinced by these conversations that this was a better route. Next spring he could travel from California to the east, intercept the emigrants west of the Rockies and lead them by a better way. He would be a hero, a leader who could then convince them to follow him in a war to take California from Mexico.

Hastings was ambitious but he was not a fool. He had successfully led the Hastings-White party to Oregon in 1842, and he led another party from Oregon to California the following year. He was a lawyer and had written a guide-book about Oregon and California. The Hastings Cutoff was supposed to be a 100 to 300 mile short cut, and well-watered, with plenty of feed. With the intelligent, persuasive Hastings to guide them, it is no wonder that many chose to follow.

The Donner party was not the only one to follow this new route, as so many readers believe. There were approximately sixty wagons ahead of the Donner party, as well as a pack train led by the well-known Edward Bryant. Hastings was leading these groups, and they went through Nevada and over the Sierra Nevada without any unusual trouble. Because of misunderstandings, poor advice, and lack of strong leadership, the Donner party was almost hopelessly delayed before they got started.

Hastings' cutoff was not used extensively after 1846, although some parties, especially pack trains, continued to take it in subsequent years. The route was not a success, and Hastings did not succeed in fulfilling his dreams of becoming a great leader. His route, however, marked another chapter in the western migration and was instrumental in the epic tragedy of the Donner party's deaths in the Sierra Nevada. The real trouble on the Hastings Cutoff for the Donner party was encountered in Utah, before reaching Nevada. The Wasatch Mountains were very difficult to get through. If they had not spent so much time getting through these mountains the Donners probably would have made it over the Sierra before the big snow. After the Wasatch Mountains the Great Salt Desert had to be crossed, and this was ninety miles with no water. The first water was the springs at Pilot Peak.

After leaving Pilot Peak the emigrants traveled for three to four days

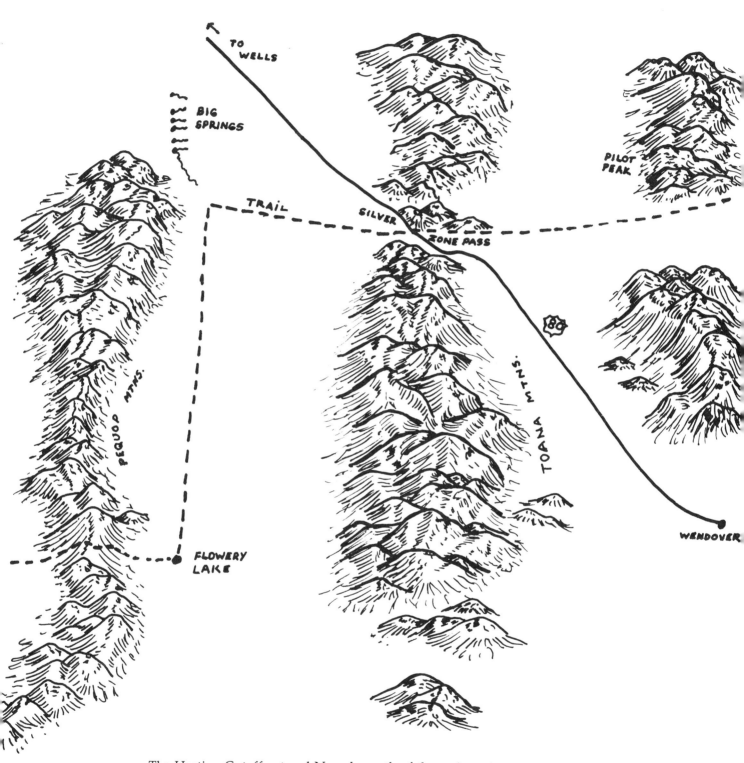

The Hasting Cutoff entered Nevada south of the main emigrant trail. This is the trail the Donner Party followed after their long journey across the Great Salt Desert.

The Nevada section of the Hasting Cutoff was easy traveling; water and grass were good.

Historical marker with Pilot Peak in the background.

through barren country, but there was enough water and feed and it did not present any great obstacle to them:

This morning we traveled over one of the most uninhabitable parts of God's Creation; not a thing but the bare earth to be seen but I suppose if it were not for these there would be no pretty places. We traveled on until 10 o'clock when we reached some water, nothing but a deep hole dug in the side of the road.

John Wood (1850)

The trail from Pilot Peak went west through Silver Zone Pass, where Highway 80 and the Western Pacific Railroad cross the Toana Range of mountains. Then it headed to the springs on the Big Springs Ranch. It was near these springs that the first party attempting to take wagons to California abandoned them.

The trail then went south to Flowery Lake, which the diarist of the Donner party, James Frazier Reed, called "Mad Womens Camp":

Left the Basin Camp or Mad Womens Camp as all the women were mad with anger and made this day to the two mound springs 14

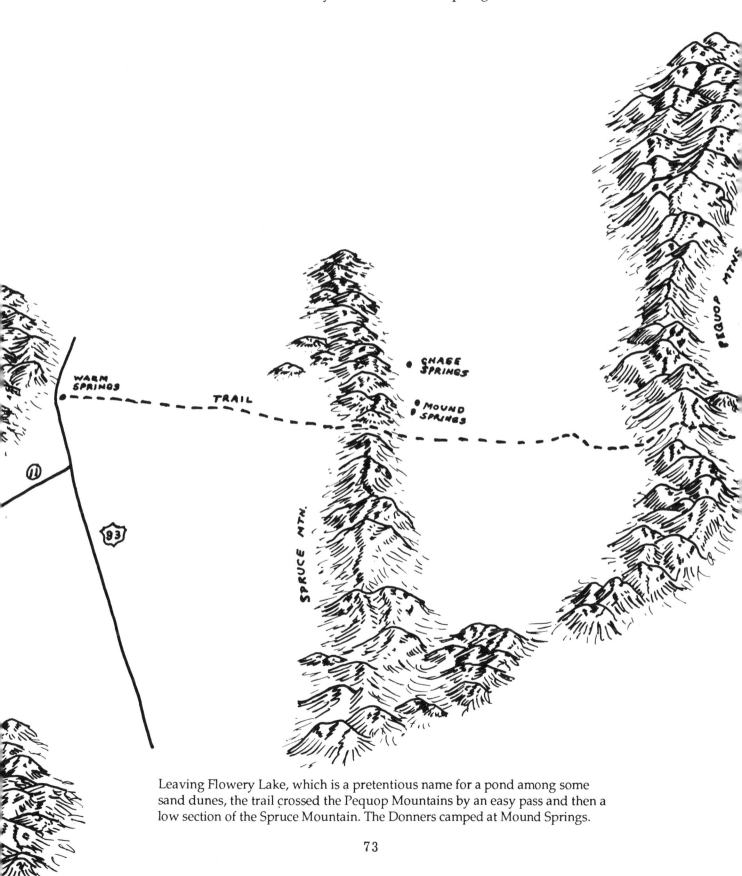

Leaving Flowery Lake, which is a pretentious name for a pond among some
sand dunes, the trail crossed the Pequop Mountains by an easy pass and then a
low section of the Spruce Mountain. The Donners camped at Mound Springs.

73

After leaving Flowery Lake the trail crossed the
Pequop Mountains by the pass in the upper center
of the picture.

From Flowery Lake, Hastings' cutoff continued west through a gap in the Pequop
Mountains, where the Western Pacific Railroad has a tunnel, to Mound Springs.
Leaving Mound Springs, the trail crossed the northern part of the Spruce
Mountains and continued in a westerly direction to Warm Springs and then in a
southwesterly direction into the north end of Ruby Valley.

Entering the north end of Ruby Valley the emigrants saw ahead of them
both a beautiful valley and the very high Ruby Mountains:

> *Today our road led in a southwesterly direction through*
> *the valley. The mountains which we are approaching*
> *rose steep and high above the flat valley. From the*
> *foot of these mountains many beautiful cool sweet water*
> *springs have their source.*
>
> Heinrich Lienhard (1846)

The emigrants had different names for Ruby Valley, such as Valley of Fountains,
Thousand Springs Valley, Spring Valley, Fountain Valley, and Mineral Valley.
All agreed it was a lovely place:

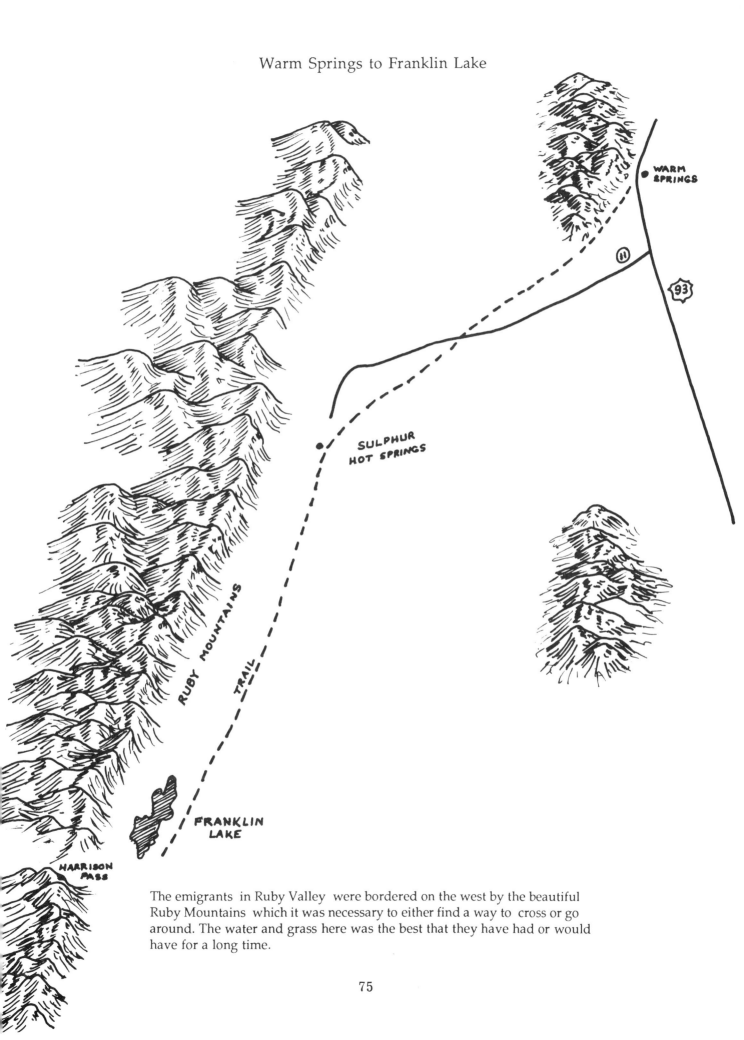

WARM SPRINGS

⑪

93

SULPHUR HOT SPRINGS

RUBY MOUNTAINS

TRAIL

FRANKLIN LAKE

HARRISON PASS

The emigrants in Ruby Valley were bordered on the west by the beautiful Ruby Mountains which it was necessary to either find a way to cross or go around. The water and grass here was the best that they have had or would have for a long time.

We are now about to start into a valley of a Thousand
Springs; the beginning looks beautiful. We started
out and traveled due south all day; about 25 miles
through one of the most beautiful and fertile valleys
I ever saw. It far exceeds Salt Lake Valley, being
more extensive and better watered; the grass is like
a meadow and the springs are innumerable. It is about
100 miles long and 30 wide, and the soil is exceedingly
rich, but there is but little timber, which is skrubby
pine, on the brow of the mountains, which surround the
valley.

John Wood (1850)

Looking south in Ruby Valley with southern
part of Ruby Mountains on the right.

In Ruby Valley some of the emigrants camped at a spring coming out of a
cave, which they called Cave Creek. The water from this spring is still called
by that name. The Ruby Valley Refuge headquarters is located on it. Both
spring and cave have been the object of many stories, some weird ones originating
with the soldiers stationed at Fort Ruby to the south. In the early 1930's a boat
was put in the cave and the water in it was explored for a distance of over seven

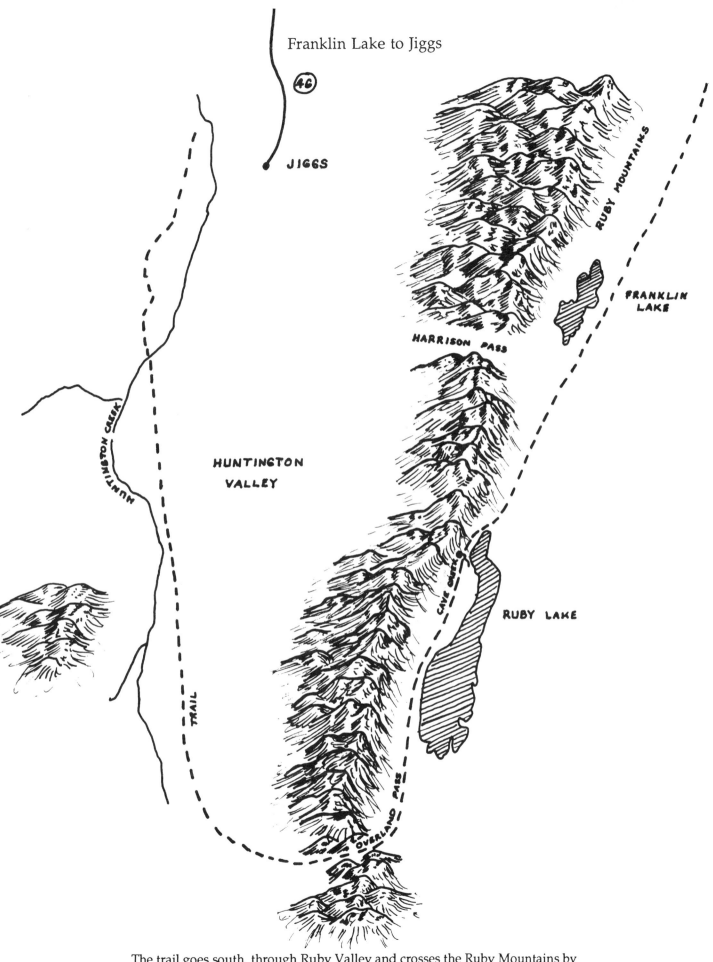

Franklin Lake to Jiggs

The trail goes south through Ruby Valley and crosses the Ruby Mountains by
Overland Pass (Hasting Pass). The pass is not long, steep or rocky. Harrison
Pass to the north could not be crossed with wagons.

hundred feet. The Donner party camped near Cave Creek:

This day made [?] in Mineral Valley 16[?] and encamped
at a large spring gushing out of from the under [?]
part of large Rock Stream large enough to turn one
pr [?] stone . . .

James Frazier Reed (1846)

Cave Creek in Ruby Valley.
The Donner party camped near here in 1846.

Hastings' trail went down Ruby Valley to the south end of the Ruby Mountains, then due west over a low pass that was very easy to ascend. This is now called Overland Pass:

The road made a turn to the right over the mountains,
in a very nearly due west course. The pass is an
excellent one - no rocks - not very steep and the
road very firm. Right on the summit is a spring
of only tolerable water.

Madison B. Moorman (1850)

Overland Pass.
Looking west into Huntington Valley.

The higher we went, however, the more the road veered
to the right. Having reached the gap shortly afternoon,
we stopped for lunch because there were several springs
nearby. Continuing on our way, we came through an open
grove of white alders.

Heinrich Lienhard (1846)

Having traveled south in Ruby Valley, then seven miles west over Overland Pass, the emigrants now traveled north through Huntington Valley to the Humboldt River near the town of Elko. This long detour was the only way for wagons to get over the Ruby Mountains. There was a pass on the north end of the Ruby Mountains - Secret Pass - but this could be used only by pack trains. Near the middle of the mountains was another pass - Harrison Pass - which was too steep for wagons.

On the cutoff, as on the main trail, information about routes was often deceiving. In Ruby Valley, one group thought they were near Walker Lake:

We all expected to be in the mines in less than a week! - being convinced from careful examination of Fremont's Map that we were near Walkers Lake. All agreed that we were not more than one hundred and twenty five miles off and that one hundred and fifty miles was the ultimate.

Madison B. Moorman (1850)

After crossing Overland Pass the emigrants made an easy descent to Huntington Creek:

Just at dark we stopped and encamped on a little clear rivulet - a tributary of the South Fork of the St. Mary's or Humboldt River, coursing its way to the North through a fertile valley well set with grass.

Madison B. Moorman (1850)

Looking north in Huntington Valley
along Huntington Creek.

The emigrants followed Huntington Creek to its junction with the South Fork of the Humboldt River. Near here they discovered a soap mine:

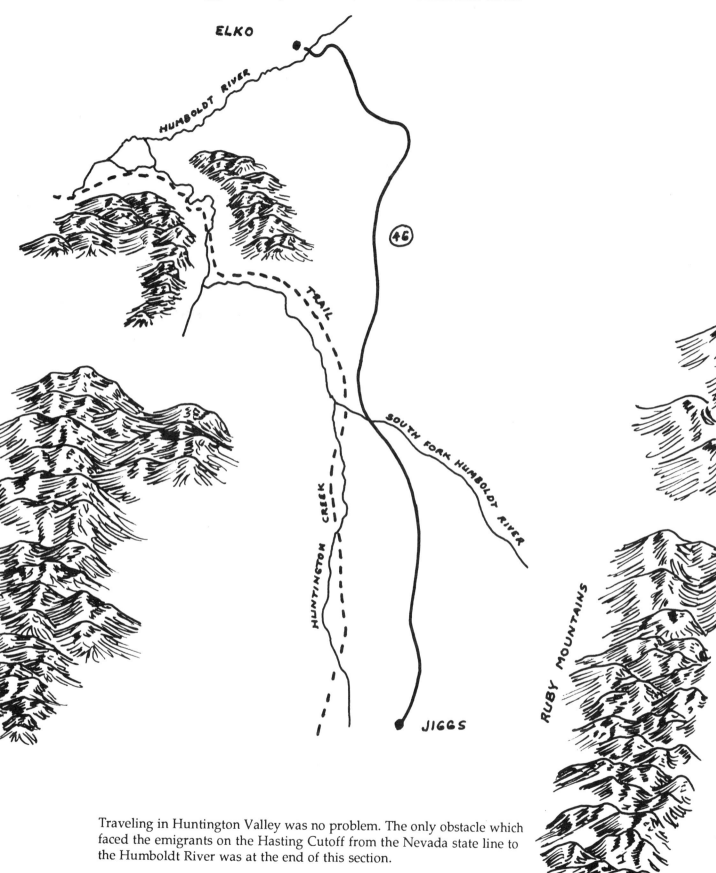

Traveling in Huntington Valley was no problem. The only obstacle which faced the emigrants on the Hasting Cutoff from the Nevada state line to the Humboldt River was at the end of this section.

They had to follow the South Fork of the Humboldt through a narrow winding canyon with the trail in the bed of the steam for much of the way. The Donners camped in this canyon.

81

*In the bank of the creek where it angled to the West
we discovered a soap mine, there seemed to be any
quantity of this substance - As good a soap as ever
was made.*

Madison B. Moorman (1850)

The emigrants' soap mine
on the South Fork of the Humboldt River.

The emigrants had some trouble with the Indians in Huntington Valley, but the most annoying part of the travel on this section was a deep, rugged canyon on the north end:

*As I approached the mountains before me, I could see
a new deep canyon with rocks rising perpendicular on
both sides. The course of the stream and our road
led in that direction.*

Heinrich Lienhard (1846)

This canyon is six miles long, and for wagons there was nowhere to go except right in the bed of the stream:

*Hardly two hundred paces from the campsite we entered
the deep canyon through which the stream had cut its
course and along which our road led. In many places*

the rock walls rose almost perpendicular; the stream made many bends, now to the right, now to the left. As the canyon narrowed, we were often under the impression that there was no outlet until we were almost upon it. . . . We had to keep crossing the stream with the water often almost reaching the wagon bed. In other places, we had to go almost straight down into the river three, four or five feet from the bank, only to go up just as steep an embankment on the other side. In this way, we crossed the river thirteen times, and late in the afternoon we arrived at the last crossing.

Heinrich Lienhard (1846)

Entrance to the canyon on the South Fork
of the Humboldt River.

Sometimes those on horseback or muleback would travel along the very steep sides:

We entered a very rugged kanyon of six or seven miles continuance. We crossed four or five times the, here very rapid and deep little river, and sometimes, to avoid a crossing, we would leave the wagon track and

risk a hazardous bridle way on the steep and rugged
mountain side, from which an awkward step of our sure
footed mules would have hurled us a hundred feet and
launched us in the river foaming in the depth below.
                    Madison B. Moorman (1850)

The winding canyon of the South Fork.
The emigrants had to take their wagons right down the river.

Emerging from this canyon the emigrants were a short distance from the
Humboldt River and the main emigrant trail. This was the end of the Hastings
Cutoff; those using this route would discover that they had lost time by taking
it. Others who went by the regular route were far ahead of them:

> *Near sunset crossed the river, near the place where*
> *emigrants route, called "Hasting's Cutoff" forms a*
> *junction with our road. . . At this encampment, I*
> *have conversed with a number of men who have just*
> *come through by way of Hasting's Cut-Off, or rather*
> *"Cut-On," as they term it, and they give it as their*
> *opinion, that it is a longer route than the northern*
> *one, by more than fifty miles.*
>   Franklin Langworthy (1850)

The Donner party, traveling this route in 1846, followed the wagon tracks of those who had gone before. By the time they emerged from the cutoff they knew that they were in trouble. They had lost a lot of time on the Wasatch Mountains and the Great Salt Desert, their food supply was becoming depleted, the animals were weakening, and worst of all, their spirit was broken. Some historians maintain that it was at this junction of the Humboldt River and the Hastings Cutoff that they sent two of their party ahead to Sutter's Fort, to obtain supplies and return. Others say it was further back on the trail. The two men were William McCutchen and Charles Stanton. The latter, who would later meet his death in the snows, returned with the supplies and met the Donner party on the Truckee River.

South Fork of Humboldt to Carlin

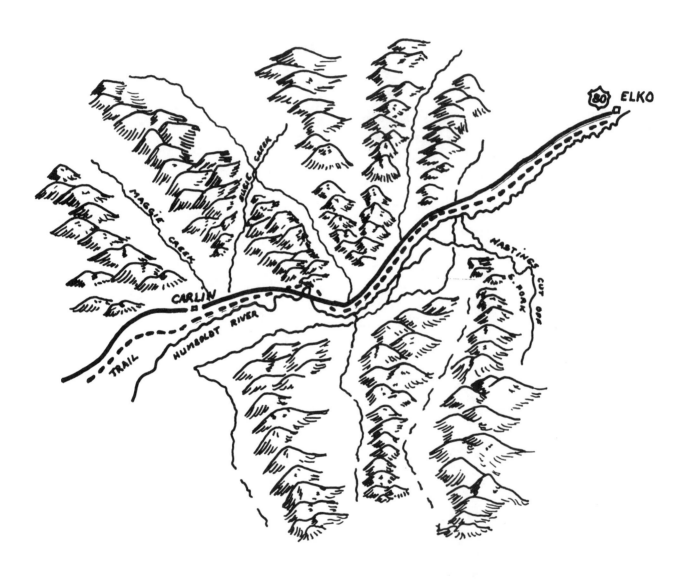

A few miles from the junction of the south fork and the Humboldt River the emigrants came to Carlin Canyon. This canyon was not difficult to travel through and as the river went through it, most of them followed the river, some were misled and detoured around by the "Greenhorn Cutoff."

V. On the Humboldt: From the South Fork
to Lassen Meadows

Carlin Canyon.

Beginning at that point where the South Fork - or the Hastings Cutoff - joined the main Humboldt River, all the emigrants found themselves traveling the same route. Just a few miles west of where the Hastings Cutoff and the main trail met, the emigrants came to Carlin Canyon. Here they had a decision to make: to go through or around the canyon. Most of them went through, but some took the "Greenhorn Cutoff" around the canyon. The latter came down Susie Creek and joined the others just east of the town of Carlin.

The Donners traveled the canyon road, as James Frazier Reed noted: "Came through a short cannon and encamped above the first creek (after cannon) on Mary's River." This entry was made on Sunday, September 27. All the miles ahead of them and the lateness of the season, increased the Donners' anxiety and made the long journey down the Humboldt more difficult.

Shortly after passing the present site of Carlin, the emigrants faced another obstacle - Palisade Canyon. This is a rugged canyon and most of the emigrants made the long and difficult detour around it over part of the Tuscarora Range. The trail parallels the present Highway 80 on the south side:

> *The mountains we are crossing today stands at right angles with our road and cuts the valley of the Humboldt into two separate divisions, making an upper and lower Humboldt Valley.*
>
> *We camped tonight on the summit of this great mountain; tired, hungry and disappointed, we pitch our tents besides a spring of good water, but of so scant a volume that we can give no drink to our thirsty and half famished animals. This has been a hard afternoon to ourselves and teams; seven miles of a continuous rise and many places so abrupt that it took all the strength of men and teams to overcome the difficulties of the way.*
>
> John Hawkins Clark (1852)

Palisade Canyon.
Most of the emigrants made a long detour
around this canyon.

> *Crossed Cold Creek and in 1½ miles commenced ascending*
> *a very long steep hill upon what is 17 miles stretch*
> *without water. We found springs in several places if*
> *they were cleaned out and taken care of would afford*
> *plenty of water but loose stock being permitted to*
> *run through them they are nothing but mud holes now*
> *affording water to neither man or beast the road is*
> *very rough and stony through this long stretch.*
> James B. Brown (1859)

The springs encountered on this detour are still called Emigrant Springs and the pass on the highway is named Emigrant Pass. Some of the emigrants did not take the detour and went through Palisade Canyon without difficulty:

> *After arriving at our camp we found we had made a*
> *great mistake in coming so far around the bluff.*
> *It was one, how-ever, that all the emigrants had*
> *made before us. Some of our men followed the river*
> *up & came to our camping place 4 hours before us,*
> *it being only 8 miles. They describe it as being*
> *as good a road for wagons as any we have seen,*
> *requiring to cross the river twice, but good*
> *crossing.*
> Vincent Geiger (1849)

After leaving the springs or emerging from Palisade Canyon, the next main camp was Gravelly Ford:

> *We left the Humboldt River and struck across the hills*
> *for a stretch of eighteen or twenty miles, through*
> *dusty and rough hills and down cannons, and after a*
> *weary march of all day and part of the night, we*
> *came to the Humboldt River again at a point known as*
> *Gravelly Ford.*
> Thomas Cramer (1859)

> *Traveled over a tremendous mountain and through*
> *canion 20 miles without grass or water and camped*
> *on humboldt crossed gravely ford.*
> Unknown, Virginia City Fire House
> Diary

Gravelly Ford was named because of the gravel in the river bed that made a good crossing for the wagons. It is located east of the town of Beowawe and has become well known in Nevada history because of the Maiden's Grave. The Maiden's Grave has been sentimentally linked with Gravelly Ford ever since the tracks of the Central Pacific Railroad were laid there.

The facts about this grave, like many other aspects of the emigrant

Carlin to Beowawe

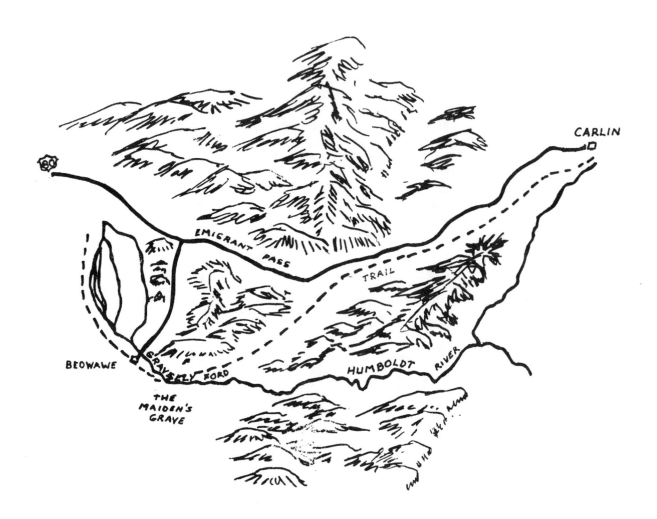

The first part of the detour around Palisade Canyon was difficult as it was a long uphill climb without water. There were springs at the summit and from there to Gravelly Ford it was not difficult to travel. This detour was over part of the Tuscarora Range.

Pioneer grave at Gravelly Ford.

Pioneer graves at Gravelly Ford.

trail, have been disputed; but all agree that the person buried in it is Lucinda Duncan. According to the *Pacific Tourist Guide:*

> *There is hardly an old resident on this coast, but who has some incident to relate in reference to Gravelly Ford. It was not only an excellent crossing place, but it was also a fine camping place, where both man and beast could recruit . . .*
>
> *On a low point of land that juts out toward the river on the south side of the track (Central Pacific) and just below this ford, is the Maidens Grave.*
>
> *Tradition has it that she was one of a party of emigrants from Missouri, and that, at this ford, while they were in camp, she sickened and died . . .*
>
> *The railroad builders came along, and found the low mound, and the decayed headboard . . . they made a new grave & surrounded it with an enclosure - a picket fence, painted white and by the side of it erected a cross . . . which bears on one side, this legend - "The Maidens Grave" and on the other her name, "Lucinda Duncan."*

The Southern Pacific Railroad version, told in one of their bulletins, is as follows:

> *Just outside Beowawe, Nevada, on a hill covered with twisted sagebrush there is a grave - The Maidens Grave.*
>
> *The story of Lucinda Duncan, the young maiden who was laid to rest on this lonely hill, is a legend in railroading and Nevada history. And, as in all legends, many questions remain unanswered.*
>
> *How old was Lucinda? Some of the old timers say 13, others add a few years but most agree she was in her teens . . . .*
>
> *When the men of our railroad, (the Central Pacific) were building the Overland Route, they noticed the grave near the track site. On a small marker beside it was carved only the name - Lucinda Duncan.*
>
> *The men - among them Indians who worked for us - cleaned the area around the grave and surrounded it with a white picket fence. They constructed a cross and inscribed on one side of it - "The Maidens Grave" and on the other, her name. From that time on, the section gangs took special interest in the solitary grave besides the track. They kept it clean, and from time to time they would pick flowers & bring them to the grave, a tribute to the young*

*pioneer maiden whose journey ended before she reached
the promised land of California.*

*In 1906 when the Old Central Pacific route was
realigned, it was found the new route would pass
directly through the grave area. Again doing the
gentle thing, our men moved the maidens grave to a
small pioneer cemetery located on a hill a few hundred
yards from the track.*

*By this time the story of the "Maidens Grave" had
become a legend, not only to the railroaders but to
the travelers riding our trains along the Overland
Route. Conductors pointed out the little cemetery
to passengers and told them the story of Lucinda
Duncan. The stories weren't always the same but
that doesn't matter - imagination is the soul of
legend.*

*It was not long before the railroaders' devoted care
of Lucinda's grave became a part of the legend, but
the S. P. men did not stop caring for the grave. In
1950 they decided to replace the aged cross with a
large one which could be seen easily by passengers
on our trains.*

The next two stories change the legend and the occupant of the grave
from a maiden to a grandmother:

*Lucinda Duncan was my grandmother. I have known the
story of her death all my life. I heard it from my
mother, Melinda Duncan Thompson Robertson and from
my half sisters. All who told it to me were on the
wagon train with Lucinda coming west to California
in the spring of 1863. I have told it several times
to feature writers and it has been published once or
twice. My story has never replaced the legend.
Lucinda Duncan was not a girl of 17 or 18. She was
a grandmother of 70 and she died near the Humboldt
River with her children & grandchildren about her . . . .*

*There were 40 wagons that left Missouri that spring -
all Duncans . . . . My grandmother, Lucinda Duncan,
headed the wagons, she was the revered one and they
gave her the place of honor. Then too, they knew
there would be less dust at the head of the train . . . .*

*I do not know the date my grandmother died but I
do know what killed her. It was an aneurism of the
heart.*

                                    Iva Rader

An event occured last night that has cast a gloom over our camp; the death of one of its members. An old lady, the mother and grandmother of a large part of our train . . . . she was pious and beloved by the whole train, relatives & strangers. Her relatives took her death very hard . . . . Before leaving camp Mrs. Duncan's funeral was preached by Capt. Peterson. Her remains was carried to its last resting place as we proceeded on our journey & up on a high point to our left about one mile from camp, we paid our last debt & respect to the remains of the departed mother. There upon that wild & lonely spot, we left her, until Gabriel shall sound his trumpet in the last day. The scene was truely a sad one to leave a beloved mother on the wild & desolate plains. A board with the name of the deceased was put up at the head & boulders was laid over the grave to keep wolves from scratching in it.

James Pressley Yager (1863)

Whether she was a maiden or a grandmother makes no difference. That tall cross still stands over the grave and looks down on the Humboldt River, to remind us of the sacrifice that many made in crossing this land.

The Maiden's Grave.

After leaving Gravelly Ford the trail was again sometimes on the bluffs and sometimes in the bottoms, but detours around canyons became fewer as it went down the valley. As grass became scarcer the emigrants made many "camp roads" looking for it, and this maze of roads sometimes led to confusion:

> *Each one started off when & where as he pleased*
> *scattering the company in every direction, for*
> *there seemed to be no regular road - wagons*
> *having run all over the country in search of*
> *grass.*
>
> Madison B. Moorman (1850)

The emigrants were now opposite the present town of Battle Mountain, at Stony Point:

> *Traveled along the river till near noon, when we*
> *reached Stony Point. At this point the hills*
> *approach to the river and the road winds around the*
> *foot for a quarter of a mile, is very rough and*
> *sideling.*
>
> Velina A. Williams (1853)

Stony Point.
The Indians were very troublesome on this section of the trail.

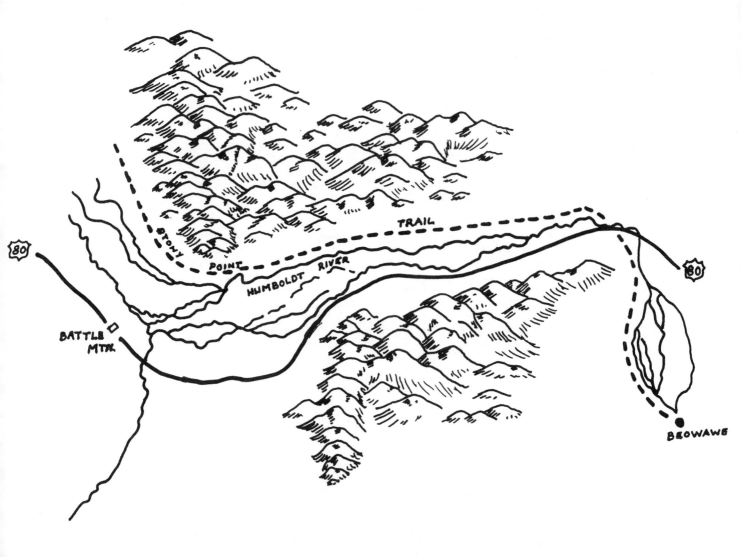

The Indians could be troublesome on this part of the trail, although this is Shoshoni territory and they were relatively peaceful. The river begins to run slower and meanders through flat country.

After passing Stony Point the country became more desert-like. It continued for most of the rest of the way like Velina Williams described it: "Traveled through a alkali region all day. The soil resembles ashes that have been leached."

Many of the emigrants traveled in pack trains, some starting that way and others abandoning their wagons when their supplies were gone or their oxen or mules stolen or dead. These pack trains could make shortcuts on the trail that the wagons couldn't follow, so in many places there was more than one trail. This was undoubtedly true on crossing Iron Point. The wagons crossed the point and then traveled down Emigrant Canyon, while the pack trains could take a straight course to the present town of Golconda:

> The country on left and ahead nearly dead level; the
> trail following the river, and the dust from the
> numerous trains indicitating [indicating] their
> extensive circuit, I determined to cut across, to
> my left, and thereby save travelling around an arc
> 6 or 7 miles longer, than by this chord. There was
> a slight horse trail across, and I wheel'd my train
> short to left, and went it.
> J. Goldsborough Bruff (1849)

From Golconda to the end of the river, the valley of the Humboldt became wider and there were no more difficult canyons. Soon the emigrants came to the big bend of the Humboldt, near Winnemucca.

The country from the town of Winnemucca down to the Lovelock Valley, where the river ended, was a torturous stretch for most emigrants. They probably suffered more on this section than anywhere else along the river. They had now been on the Humboldt for over 200 miles. Their supplies were low, feed for the stock was very scarce, they encountered more sand, water became worse, and the dust was unbearable.

There was one exception, thirty-five miles west of Winnemucca. There, a short distance northwest of the present town of Imlay, they came to a large meadow with good feed. This was called Lassen Meadows or Lawson's Meadow, and some place the "Big Bend" of the Humboldt here, rather than upstream at Winnemucca. Lassen Meadows was a desert oasis for the emigrants as there was plenty of grass for all:

> In 5 or 6 miles this morning we came to Lawson's
> Meadow here we found a little better feed than we

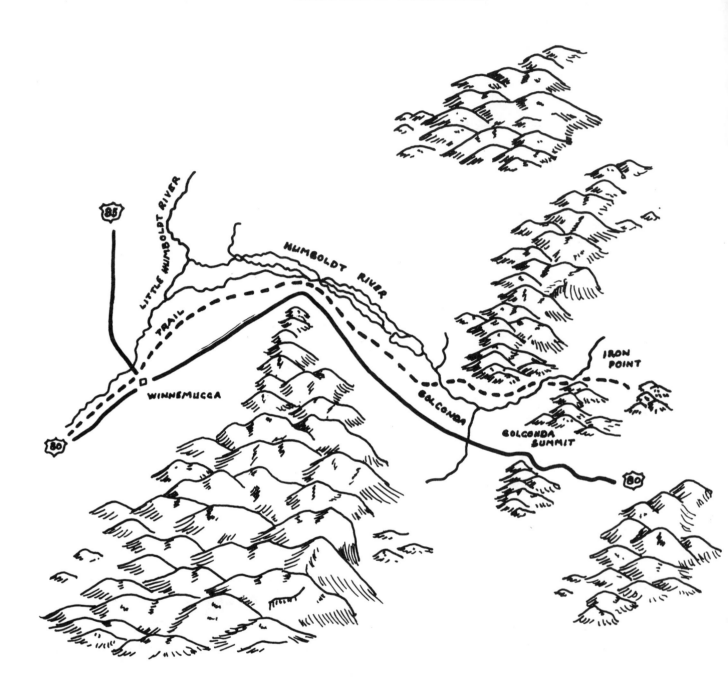

Emigrant Canyon was the last canyon which the emigrants traveled through until they reached the Truckee River or Woodsford Canyon on the Carson River route.

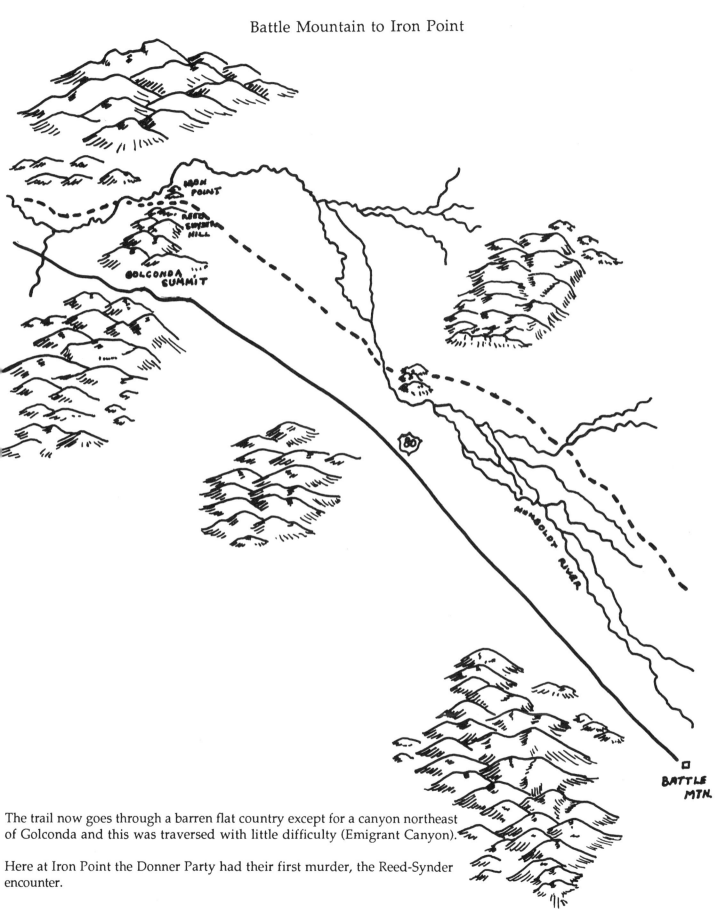

The trail now goes through a barren flat country except for a canyon northeast of Golconda and this was traversed with little difficulty (Emigrant Canyon).

Here at Iron Point the Donner Party had their first murder, the Reed-Synder encounter.

99

have had for some time being covered as usual with
salt and alkali. We camped for the day here to
recruit and cut grass . . . . The Honey Lake route
over the Sierra Nevada's comes in here.

James B. Brown (1859)

We had arrived at Lawson's Meadows . . . Instead of
wind, dust, alkali, sagebrush and greasewood, we
found ourselves in a perfect little paradise
surrounded by green grass and willows, the moon and
stars shining sweetly above us.

Harriet S. Ward (1853)

Nevada's first postal service was here:

On the right about one hundred yds. from the Bend,
the Desert Route branches off, and in the forks of
the road, I observed a red painted barrel standing -
I rode up, to examine it - It was a nice new barrel,
about the size of a whiskey-barrel, iron hoops, and
a square hole cut in the head; and neatly painted in
black letters, upon it, "Post Office."

On looking in, I found it half full of letters, notes,
notices, &c. Near this was a stick and bill board,
also filled with notices - These were chiefly directed
to emigrants in the rear, hurrying them along, giving
information about the route, telling who had taken
this or the southern route, &c. By these I
ascertained that few had taken the southern road.

J. Goldsborough Bruff (1849)

We continued 2 miles when we came to the forks of the
road, the right hand road being what is termed the
Oregon road, a large amount of Emigration had taken
this road to avoid the mountains the distance by
this road is nearly 200 miles further than the left
hand road, we took the left hand. at the forks of
the road was a post office consisting of a large
water cask it had a large amount of communications
in it.

David DeWolf (1849)

The grass of Lassen Meadows was good and plentiful, but this was also
a place where many left the trail forever:

A man drowned here this morning while crossing the
river on a mule. Mule stepped in a deep hole. Man
got off and was drowned. Dragged river most all
day but did not find him . . . . The sick are better.
Had cholera and mountain fever.

Andrew Soule (1854)

Winnemucca to Lassen Meadows

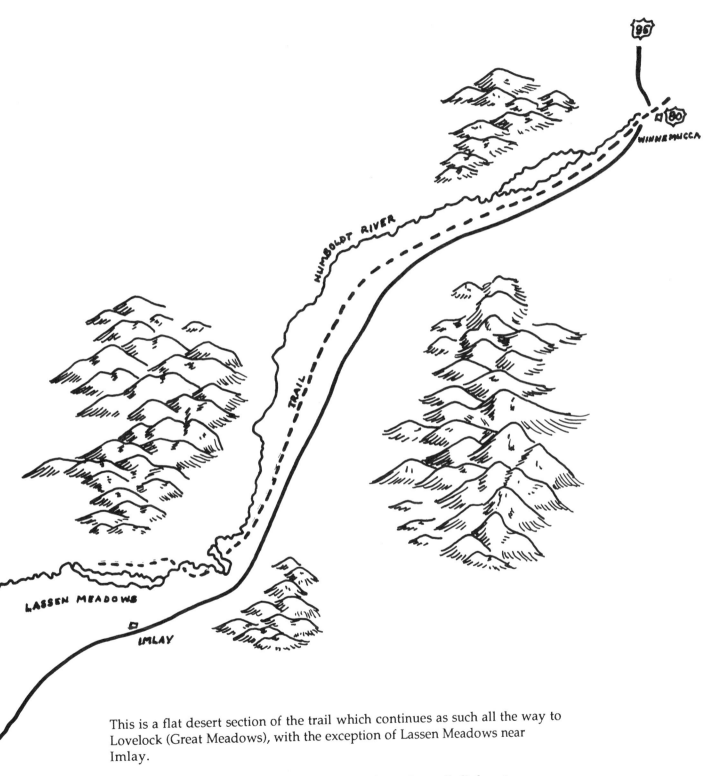

This is a flat desert section of the trail which continues as such all the way to Lovelock (Great Meadows), with the exception of Lassen Meadows near Imlay.

The Humboldt River slowly works its way through an alkali desert.

Here was many emigrants in camp. Five had died during
the night, & one man just drowned in bringing the
stock over . . . . Graves are very plenty all along
here & the dead stock make you sick, the stench is so
great.

John Clark of Virginia (1852)

Lassen Meadows was a place to prepare for that long, dry, grassless stretch to the Great Meadows near Lovelock. It was also the place where the road to Oregon and northern California left the main California trail:

Reached the meadows about 4 o'clock and pitched our
tents for the last time on the banks of the Humboldt
River. The grass here is on the south side of the
river and grows in abundance.

Velina A. Williams (1853)

Here the Lawson Trail bears off to Shasty. When we
came to the forks of road, the left being the old
road to California; going into same through the great
pass in the mountains and right leading further north,
near Mud Lake and striking the head of Feather River.
The majority of the emigrants having taken this road
we concluded to try the experiment and soon commenced
ascending the gradual slope to the pass in the mountains.

John E. Brown (1849)

The trail referred to here is the Applegate Trail that went into Oregon. It was later known as the Applegate-Lassen Trail when a branch of it was opened into California. The Applegate-Lassen Trail left the main trail between Winnemucca and Lovelock, and headed in a northwesterly direction across the northern part of Washoe County into Oregon and California.

VI. The Applegate Trail

In 1846, a group of men headed by Jesse Applegate left the Willamette Valley in Oregon to find a better way for emigrants to reach that valley. The established trail to Oregon was down the Snake and Columbia Rivers to the Dalles; here the wagons had to be left or the emigrants had to float them down the Columbia River on rafts, which was very dangerous. Applegate and his men succeeded in reaching the Humboldt River on a route that they considered a good one, by which wagons could be taken all the way to the Willamette Valley. They established the turning-off point on the Humboldt River at Lassen Meadows.

Peter Lassen later saw an opportunity to branch off this newly established trail to Oregon and bring emigrants by his ranch, which was near Chico, California. He used the Applegate Trail to Goose Lake, near Lakeview, Oregon; at the south end of the lake he left the Oregon Trail and headed toward the Sacramento Valley. A large number of gold seekers used this Applegate-Lassen Route into California, although it was not an improvement on the established California Trail by way of the Truckee or Carson Rivers.

Why did so many take this new route that had not been traveled or proven? It seemed safer to risk the unknown dangers of a new trail than the known dangers of the Humboldt route. The emigrants knew that from Lassen Meadows to the present town of Lovelock there was nothing but a desert - deep sand, poor water, and no grass; and they had heard horrifying stories about the Forty Mile Desert beyond Lovelock. The Sierra Nevada had to be climbed and crossed, and the tragedy of the Donner party was always on their minds. Some taking the Applegate Trail were just adventurous, but others felt the route might prove to be a good one and get them to the gold fields a little quicker:

> *The question arose which of the two roads shall we persue - follow the old road - the advantages and disadvantages of which we are pretty well informed; or shall we risk the new one of which we know nothing, except from unreliable reports.*
>
> Kimball Webster (1849)

> *A man on horseback reported that he had rode thirty miles out on the route; that in ten miles there was grass, in twelve grass and water, and in twenty, grass and water in abundance; and on reaching Rabbit Springs,*

a distance of thirty-five miles, all difficulty would
be ended. Others said that for thirty five miles
there was neither grass nor water; that the road did
not go to California at all, but to Oregon, and that
the Indians were troublesome and bad.
Alonzo Delano (1849)

Those deciding to take the Applegate-Lassen Route took the right hand
trail at the forks and left the Humboldt River and the central overland trail to
California. These emigrants then headed in a northwesterly direction across
northern Nevada:

The new road takes immediately to the desert of
fifty-five miles extent with two weak springs on the
route. We arrived at the first spring - 15 miles -
at four o'clock in the evening, took our supper and
gave our teams what water we could get and started
for the second, where we arrived at four in the
morning. Found the spring weaker than the first.
Virgil Pringle (1846)

The Applegate Trail leaving Lassen Meadows

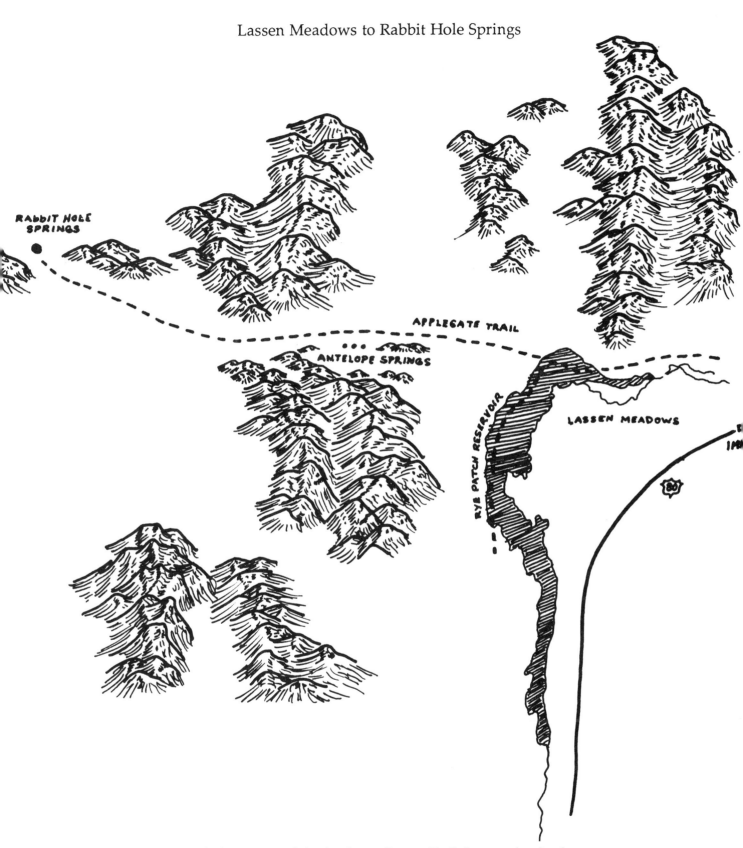

RABBIT HOLE SPRINGS

APPLEGATE TRAIL

ANTELOPE SPRINGS

RYE PATCH RESERVOIR

LASSEN MEADOWS

This is the beginning of the Applegate-Lassen Trail. It was taken by those heading for Willamet Valley in Oregon and by some emigrants who thought it was a better way to California.

*The "Cutoff" leaves the river and crosses a desert
plain, very barren and slightly undalating in a
westerly direction.*
                            Kimball Webster (1849)

*The first 4 miles was over a plain as level as a
marble-tablet, and nearly as smooth; firm, where
not cut into by the travel, white, and sun cracked.*
                            J. Goldsborough Bruff (1849)

Their first objective was Antelope Springs, a distance of fourteen miles. Here
they met with their first disappointment:

*There are 3 spring places here, in this mountain dell -
a few hundred yards apart; the centre are 3/4, and the
flankers about 1/2 mile from road on plateau . . .
These were mere dripplings percolating from small clay
cliffs in the hollow slope of the mountain.*
                            J. Goldsborough Bruff (1849)

*We encamped for the night upon the side of a mountain;
and there being neither water nor grass for our poor,
toil-worn cattle, they were carefully guarded through
the night. I had gone forward in the morning, and
found, within about three-fourth of a mile of our
encampment, and far up the side of the mountain a
very small vein of water, that moistened the ground
a few yards around.*
                            J. Quinn Thornton (1848)

After the disappointment at this first spring some of the emigrants began
to have doubts about the new route. Some even returned to the Humboldt River
to take the old route. Those continuing from the first spring traveled another
fourteen miles to Rabbit Hole Spring. Here their disappointment was compounded,
for there was very little water and the emigrants could look across a barren flat
for twenty-five miles and see nothing but the while alkali of the desert:

*Judge of our disappointment, when we found the promised
springs to be only three or four wells sunk in the
ground, into which the water percolated in a volume
about the size of a straw, and each hole occupied
by a man dipping it up with a pint cup as it slowly
filled a little cavity in the ground . . . Beyond
us, far as we could see, was a barren waste, without
a blade of grass or a drop of water for thirty miles
at least.*
                            Alonzo Delano (1849)

Later emigrants dug these springs out to increase the amount of water:

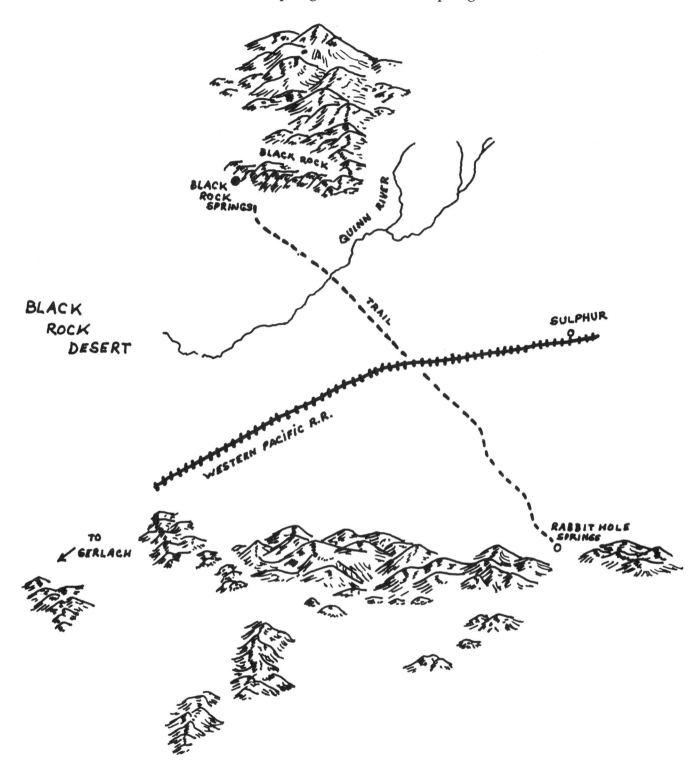

Rabbit Hole Springs was a disappointment, and water was limited. A few miles from the springs the flat, barren Black Rock Desert begins. Early maps show Quinn River on this section but in most years it is just a dry depression in this old alkali lake bed.

We came to a place known as Rabbit Wells, where four
or five wells, some 8 or 10 feet deep, have been
excavated by the emigrants in advance for the purpose
of obtaining water for themselves and their stock.
These wells, with one or two exceptions, were filled
with dead animals.

Kimball Webster (1849)

Rabbit Hole Springs.
The springs were mere trickles of water in the emigrant days.

Leaving Rabbit Hole Springs, the emigrants descended to the Black Rock Desert. Here they set their eyes on a black rock in the distance and made a straight line for it. On this desert, as on the Forty Mile Desert on the Truckee and Carson routes, many animals died and hundreds of wagons and other belongings were abandoned. The distance across the Black Rock Desert was shorter than the Forty Mile Desert on the Truckee and Carson routes. The road was harder and didn't have the deep sand that was found on the other trails, but the animals were so weak at the start of the crossing that they didn't have sufficient reserve strength to make it:

*Just as the sun was sinking, we resumed our journey
[across the Black Rock Desert], and after descending
a little hill we entered a country more forbidding
and repulsive than even that I have described. There
we occasionally saw a stray and solitary bush of
artemisia. It was a country which had nothing of a
redeeming character. Nothing presented itself to
the eye, but a broad expanse of a uniform dead level
plain, which conveyed to the mind the idea that it
had been the muddy sandy bottom of a former lake.*

J. Quinn Thornton (1848)

Grave of Susan Coon - a later emigrant.

*The scene along the road the last few days, no one
can describe and have anyone believe him. Hundreds
of dead cattle lay strung along the road and in the
road. Such a smell. It is worse by nite. Not only
the dead cattle and their smell but the discord of
men. Brother blaming each other for having lost
their teams and leaving all behind. Some divided
their teams and left their wagons, packed a few
things on their backs and walked on cursing.*

Andrew Soule (1854)

The locality was rendered none the more enticing to myself from the fact that, for miles back along the road I had come, I could have stepped almost continuously from the carcass of one dead horse or ox to another; so great had been the number of animals that had here perished from hunger, thirst and general exhaustion.
David Rohrer Leeper (1849)

The stillness of death reigns over this vast plain, - not the rustling of a leaf or the hum of an insect, to break in on the eternal solitude.
George Keller (1850)

Intense sandstorms were another of the Black Rock Desert's hazards:

Once we reached a place where two years before a party of emigrants had been surprised by a sandstorm and had perished. Remains could still be seen of oxen and horses lying in pairs and partly covered with sand; of the wagons nothing was left but wheel rims and other iron.
Tosten K. Stabaek (1852)

What the "goldseekers" left behind others soon turned into gold:

The day we crossed Rabbit Hole to Black Rock we crossed a desert of pure sand, free from all kinds of vegetation, the route plainly marked by the mummyfied remains of cattle and horses that had perished of thirst and wagons abandoned because there was no teams left to draw them. All kinds of household goods thrown away to lighten loads; and in one place, setting not far from the road, was a melodion abandoned from the same stern necessity.

I heard men who crossed that desert state it as their belief that there were enough chains left on that desert to reach, if linked together, from Black Rock to the Humboldt River. Years later, enterprising individuals went back there with large teams and wagons to gather up loads of wagon iron and chains, reaping rich returns from the enterprise.
Velina A. Williams (1853)

Years later a surveyor noted on his map of the Black Rock: "There is no place just like this place anywhere near this place so this must be the place."

After the emigrants crossed this desert they arrived at a large hot spring near the Black Rock that had been their guide:

High above the plain, in the direction of our road, a black, bare mountain reared its head, at the distance of fifteen miles.
Alonzo Delano (1849)

110

Black Rock - the emigrants guide
across the Black Rock Desert.

*Stop'd at about 8'Oclock at Hot Springs & the water
was hot enough to boil an egg & from which we made
some tea, which was so nauseous that I could hardly
drink it, accustomed as we are to drink and eat
anything. The stench and effluvia of the Springs and
the water flowing therefrom was very disagreeable.
We were glad enough to go to bed, but we were awake
the greatest part of the night by the greatest
confusion, teams after teams & pack mules constantly
arriving & all seeking for water, they continued to
arrive all hours of the night & men cursing & dogs
barking & hallooing to the oxen & children squalling,
all made a miserable time for rest.*

*Up long before sunrise & as far as we could see the
country was cover'd with oxen & mules & horses &
men & wagons, the men afoot & on horseback, all darting
and going in every direction herding up cattle who had
wander'd off in every direction for something to eat
and drink.*

                    Charles Gray (1849)

Black Rock Spring - the first water
after crossing the Black Rock Desert.

Now to say a word about the mightly sentinel of the
desert - Black Rock, many feet high, rising out of
a level plain, and from under it gushes out a boiling
hot spring with a dense fog of steam. Its bottom
can't be seen. Thirty to forty inches of water flows
from it so brackish with brimstone, you can't drink
it without feeling sick and not a green vestige can
you see. You can smell this spring for miles, and
now as I gazed on that spring, I thot of Dante's
Inferno and the Great Rock of Despair, whose waters
cannot cool it off. I have seen many hot springs
but this one can swallow them all and still flow on.
It is no wonder that this is a desert country,
destitute of any vegetation with this mightly engine
of fire so close to the surface it's life is burnt out.
                    Andrew Soule (1854)

After leaving the hot springs at the foot of the Black Rock, the trail led in a
northwesterly direction past the Double Hot Springs to Mud Lake and then
toward High Rock Canyon.

Before entering High Rock Canyon the emigrants had a very steep hill

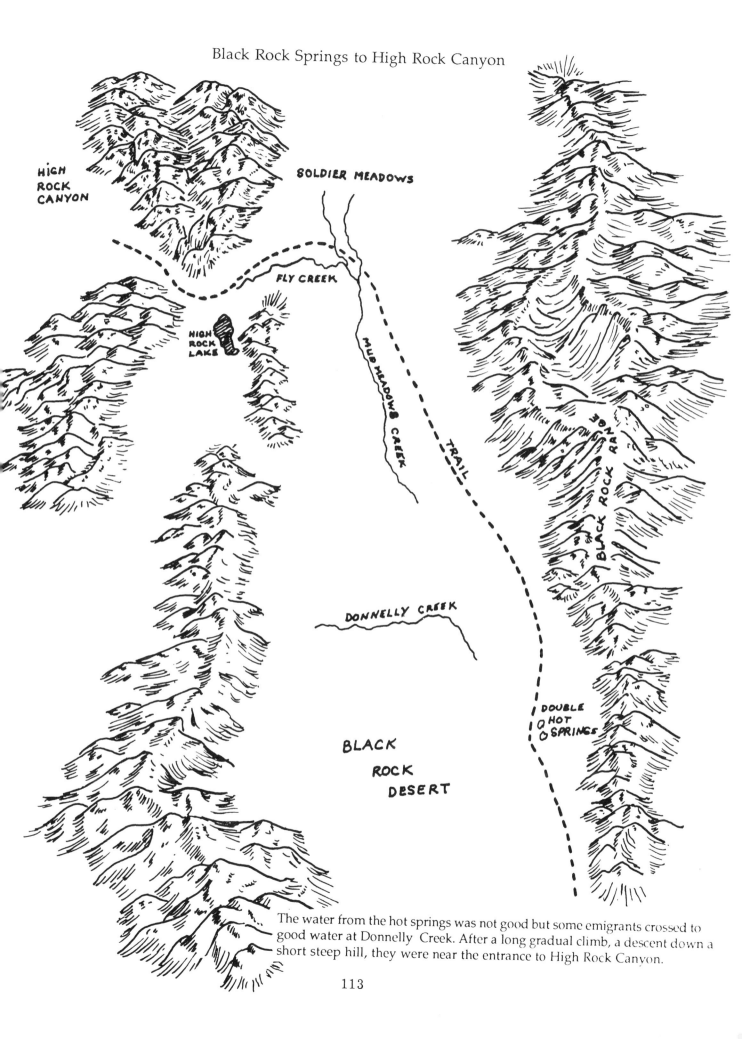

HIGH
ROCK
CANYON

SOLDIER MEADOWS

FLY CREEK

HIGH
ROCK
LAKE

MUD MEADOWS CREEK

TRAIL

BLACK ROCK RANGE

DONNELLY CREEK

DOUBLE
HOT
SPRINGS

BLACK
ROCK
DESERT

The water from the hot springs was not good but some emigrants crossed to good water at Donnelly Creek. After a long gradual climb, a descent down a short steep hill, they were near the entrance to High Rock Canyon.

Double Hot Springs.

to descend.   At the top of this hill was a brush fence that the Indians used as a snare to catch jackrabbits:

> *There was an Indian snare for catching hares. This*
> *was sage bushes, set four feet apart, propped up with*
> *stones, and extending in a line at least a mile and*
> *half over the hill as I was told by hunters who*
> *followed it.*
>
> Alonzo Delano (1849)

> *This fence was close and regular, except where travel*
> *on the road had prostrated and scattered it - was*
> *composed of sage and grease-wood bushes torn up by*
> *the roots, and placed close together, roots up.*
>
> J. Goldsborough Bruff (1849)

The steepness of the trail on this hill was changed by the Miller & Lux ranching interests and recently by the Bureau of Land Management.   A trace of the old road can be seen in the picture:

> *I came to a steep hill, down which the wagons were let*
> *with ropes into the canyon.*
>
> Alonzo Delano (1849)

114

Steep hill approaching High Rock Canyon.
A trace of the trail is in the center of the picture.
The canyon is Fly Canyon where John C. Fremont spent
New Year's Eve 1843.

*The road terminated, as it were, at the edge of the
very apex of this hill, and from a big rock on the
left of trail, at crest, I looked down, and for
awhile thought it must be "the jumping off place."*
                        J. Goldsborough Bruff (1849)

Soon the trail entered a remarkable canyon:

*Twelve miles from Mud Lake, we entered the High Rock
Canyon which possesses some features that are unique
and striking. It cuts through a range of lava that
is some twenty miles in width and bare of vegetation,
as if it had cooled but the day before. The fissure
or gorge that afforded us passage is about the width
of a common road, and is inclosed by high walls that
are carved in irregular outline as if by action of an
ancient ice river.*

                        David Rohrer Leeper (1849)

In the afternoon we passed through a defile of 2 miles length between rocks of from 3 to 500 feet high, the defile being quite narrow.

Charles Gray (1849)

We started in the morning and soon after entered a canyon and traveled 12 miles in the forenoon and halted where the rocky bluffs rise nearly 300 feet. Almost perpendicular on either side.

Kimball Webster (1849)

High Rock Canyon.
The canyon was named for these rocks.

It is fortunate that Mother Nature created this long and narrow canyon by which the Indians, John C. Fremont in his exploration of 1843-1844, and now the emigrants, had a convenient passage through this rugged country. Alonzo Delano, writing about his travel through the canyon in 1849, expresses these sentiments:

Without this singular avenue, a passage across the mountains in this vicinity would have been impossible,

*and it seemed as if Providence, forseeing the wants
of his creatures, had in mercy opened this strange
path, by which they could extricate themselves from
destruction and death.*

Here, on the face of these cliffs, many of the emigrants recorded their names.
Some of these names are no longer legible, but others have survived:

*In the face of the perpendicular wall of the right
side, at base, is a singular cave . . . . Names and
dates scratched all over the outer wall around the
mouth of the cave, and numbers within . . . The
part of the wall in which this cave is, gave name to
the canon. [High Rock] As over the cave it rises in
a vast spire, I judge to be 400 feet high; however not
over 50 feet higher than the adjoining continuation.*

J. Goldsborough Bruff (1849)

Emigrants' names in High Rock Canyon.

Except for occasional skirmishes with the Indians, the emigrants continued
through High Rock Canyon without much trouble:

*As we drive along the Canon, we found good grass and
water at convenient distances and traveling agreeable.*
                                    Alonzo Delano (1849)

*There is a small stream of good water and grass in
this valley. It is about twenty miles in length. A
few miles from the ravines we found a few gallons of
good vinegar, which had been left by some emigrants.
This was quite an addition to the "greens."*
                                    George Keller (1850)

At the end of High Rock the trail led through a short but very rough and
rocky passage - Upper High Rock Canyon:

*In two miles' travel we came to the upper High Rock
Canyon. As we came near the canyon we passed a spring
of fine water. It came out half up the mountain and
ran across the road. The rocks in the passage are not
as high as those in first High Rock. The roads through
it were very bad and rocky. Some of the rocks that we
drove over were half as high as the wagon wheels. We
also had to drive in a creek for some distance and
cross it several times. The crossings were also bad.
In this canyon I saw the first trees that I have seen
since we left Fort Hall. It was quaking aspens or
poplar and some of the trees were from four to six
inches in diameter.*
                                    Israel F. Hale (1849)

*Started early. When we reached the entrance to the
canon, - turning short to the right, we found that
generally the bed of the stream was unavoidably the
line of travel through this very rugged mountain pass.
This pass, for trail there was none - was filled with
stum[p]s of cotton-wood trees, large, fallen trees,
stones and rocks of every size, Dead cattle, broken
wagons & carts, wheels, axles, tires, yokes, chains
&c &c. - testimonials of its difficult character . . . . .
The grass where the trail ran was barely broke down,
so recent has this route been. - Thank Jupiter! this
incomparable (road) route, was only about 2 ms.
through!*
                                    J. Goldsborough Bruff (1849)

This canyon eventually became impassable and a longer but easier trail was
developed around it. After leaving Upper High Rock Canyon the emigrants
traveled in a northerly direction, where the exacting diarist J. Goldsborough
Bruff noted and sketched a rock formation. He called it a "singular rock."

29th Sept.

singular Rock on left of road

huge

road

J. Goldsborough Bruff (1849)

Bruff's rock as it looked 131 years later in 1980.

119

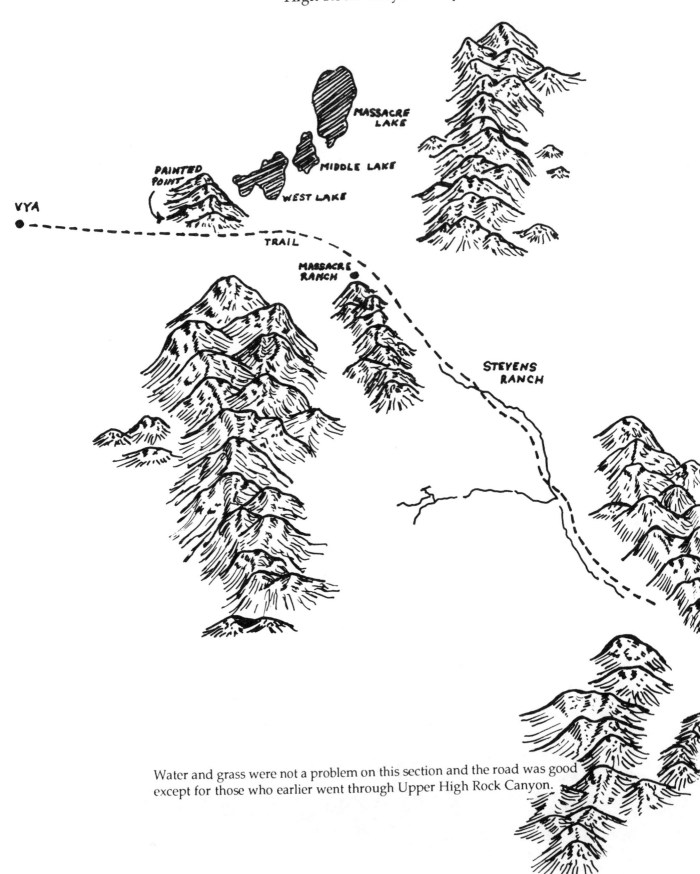

Water and grass were not a problem on this section and the road was good except for those who earlier went through Upper High Rock Canyon.

Near Bruff's rock is the massacre grave. The story of this grave remains a mystery. Was a wagon train massacred by the Indians, and all the emigrants buried in this large common grave? This has always been the story, but no one has ever found a diary to substantiate this story or any other logical explanation for the grave. In this country, however, a small group could easily have been murdered without leaving any record.

Massacre Grave near Massacre Ranch.

The trail soon turned toward the west, passing the present Washoe County Maintenance Station at Vya, then down Forty-Nine Canyon near or on the road from Vya to Cedarville, California. It then shifted to the northwest and crossed the dry lake between Cedarville and Fort Bidwell, climbing a steep mountain to Fandango Pass. Most of the emigrants did not have any trouble in reaching the summit, but there were exceptions:

> *I saw a heavy laden wagon driven by ten yoke of oxen*
> *start rapidly down the mountain. The chain attached*
> *to the tongue had broken just as they had reached the*
> *summit. It ran two or three hundred feet, taking the*

121

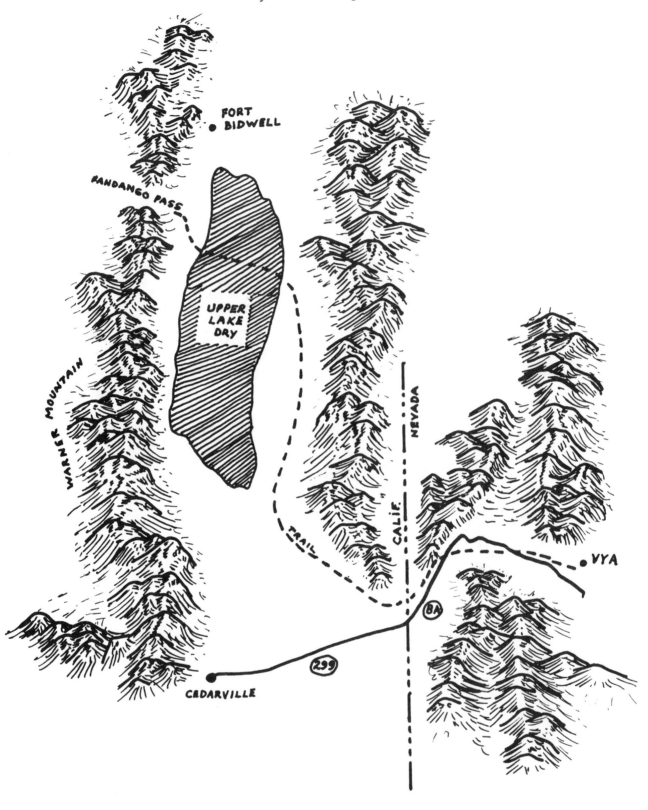

Part of the trail was very dusty but the main problem was the steep climb up
to Fandango Pass.

*wheel steers with it and luckily turned bottom
upwards. Many saw it and as many rejoiced to see
it turn over, for had it continued to follow the
road it must have destroyed considerable property,
if not some lives . . . . The dust was so great
that I did not discover oxen being fast to the wagon
until it turned over. One had broke his bow and got
loose, the other remained fast to the wagon, and you
can judge of my surprise on his being let loose to
see him jump up and run away; and how it was possible
for a yoke of oxen to be drawn backwards that distance
and with so great velocity and for neither to be
killed or crippled is something for which I cannot
account.*

Israel F. Hale (1849)

Top of Fandango Pass looking east.

Soon after leaving Fandango Pass the emigrants arrived at Goose Lake, where those going to California by the Lassen Route parted from those continuing on to Oregon.

Imlay to Lovelock (Sink)

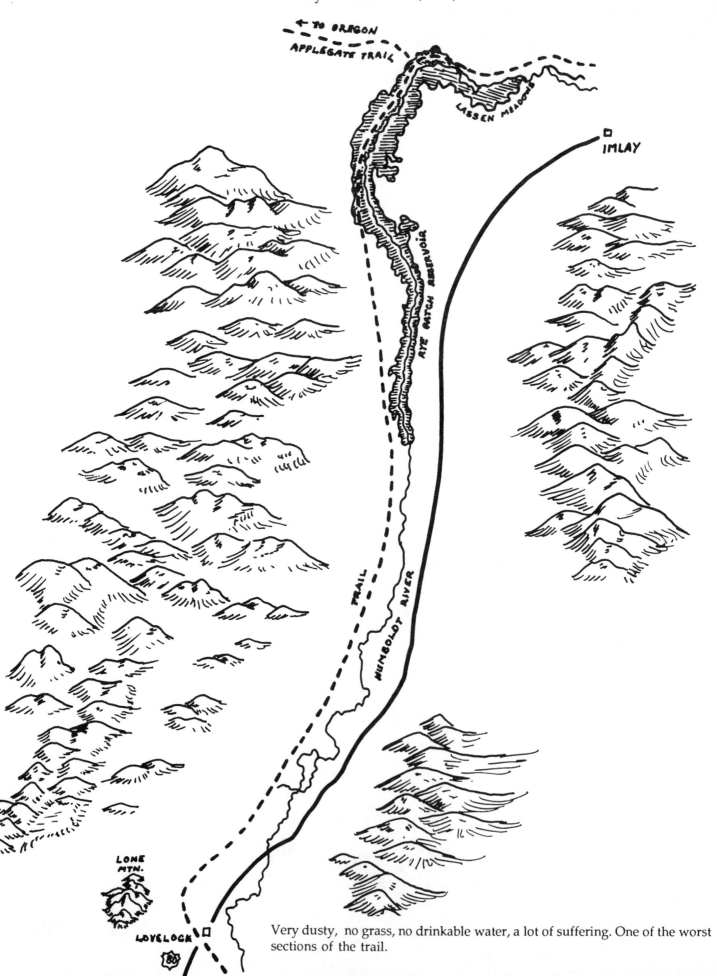

← TO OREGON

APPLEGATE TRAIL

LASSEN MEADOWS

IMLAY

RYE PATCH RESERVOIR

TRAIL

HUMBOLDT RIVER

LONE MTN.

LOVELOCK

80

Very dusty, no grass, no drinkable water, a lot of suffering. One of the worst sections of the trail.

VII. On the Humboldt:
From Lassen Meadows to the Great Meadows

At Lassen Meadows the emigrants who decided to continue on the regular route down the Humboldt River headed toward the site of present-day Lovelock, forty miles away. This section was the dustiest of the whole route, and grass and good water were almost impossible to find:

> *Today we have been toiling through the deep dust, as uncomfortable for us all as a person who has never travelled this route can ever imagine, with not a green thing to rest our weary eyes upon. It is a perfectly barren land for forty long miles, and it is distressing to hear the complaints of the poor cattle, which are suffering for want of food.*
>
> Harriet S. Ward (1853)

Lone Mountain near Lovelock, Nevada.

Suffering was the order of the day, but from a great distance the emigrants could see Lone Mountain. This was truly a mountain of hope, because near its base, in a slough, was a spring of cold water. The Great Meadows with its acres of grass and water was not far from this spring.

Even though it took some of the emigrants three days from the first sighting to reach Lone Mountain, the vision of it and the thought of cold water must have encouraged many to struggle on:

> *We are now in sight of the Pyramid, a lone peak nearly opposite the upper slough of the sink, commonly called the meadow . . . . From this it is 25 miles to the slough or meadows, and 13 to water, which will be found at some springs in the gully directly opposite the pyramid . . . The pyramid at a distance resembles an ancient Mexican pyramid, rising by steps. It may be seen for 40 miles up the river, and serves as a beacon, for the slough or meadows.*
>
> Eleazer Stillman Ingalls (1850)

The cold spring by Lone Mountain was greeted eagerly:

> *We have now traveled 3 days with little or no feed, our stock looks badly. I was never so rejoiced as when one of our men returned with a can full of good cool spring water, the first I had drunk for three weeks. We came to a cold spring at 1 o'clock. These springs are a God-sent to the poor famished emigrant.*
>
> George Willis Read (1850)

> *A fine little spring is on the opposite side of the slough, close to it the water is cold, though a little brackish or salt like (much better than river water.)*
>
> Peter Decker (1849)

> *The slue and springs mentioned on Saturday, are a short distance to left of a hill. The slue is merely a ravine, at bottom of which are several excellent springs, and not such a place as would usually be understood by the term slue.*
>
> Lorenzo Sawyer (1850)

> *We arrived at a slough, distance from the river 10 miles . . . . There is a beautiful little spring of cold water just in the edge of this slough at the right of the crossing.*
>
> Cyrus C. Loveland (1850)

After leaving the cold spring the emigrants headed toward the Great Meadows:

Lovelock to the Dike

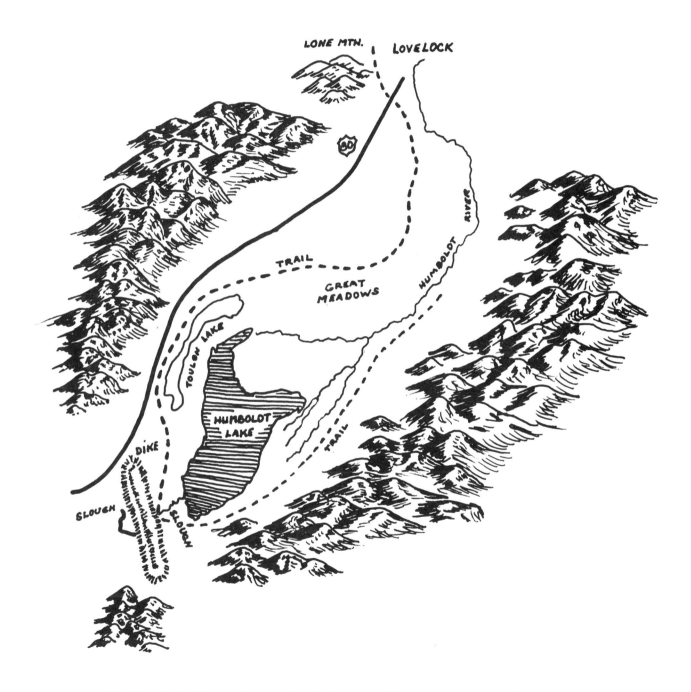

The Humboldt River ends near Lovelock, most of the emigrants referred to this area as the Sink or Great Meadows. This was the place to recruit for the challenge ahead.

From the Great Meadows to the Dike is approximately fifteen miles.

From this place we bare to the Left, go Seven miles.
Here we come to Great Meadows, near the Sink of this
River.

William H. Kilgore (1850)

Road crosses a slough, at the head of which is a
spring of cool and tolerably good water. From here
4 miles to head of a Great Meadow.

Andrew Child (1850)

Before reaching the Great Meadows, the road branched near the present site of
Lovelock. The left hand road went to the Great Meadows, and most of the
emigrants took this road. The right hand branch went by the point of a mountain
to the south, heading toward Granite Point and a direct approach to the desert:

The road forks, and the left hand turns to the Big
Slough, where there is good grass enough for all,
and plenty to spare. Straight ahead will take you
to the desert - distance 20 miles.

Dr. J. S. Shepard (1850)

Struck our camp quite early, we traveled 8 miles when
we came to the forks of the road the right hand leading
direct to sink and the left hand leading to a large
place of fine grass, etc.

David DeWolf (1849)

The left hand road leads to the river, where there is
plenty of grass . . . if you take the right hand road,
you will pass the point of a mountain, etc.

P. L. Platt (1849-1850)

The emigrants were now in the Lovelock Valley, just past the town of
Lovelock in what is presently known as the Lower Valley and what the emigrants
called the Great Meadows. This was the end of the Humboldt River. The Great
Meadows was a place of rejoicing for most; they had traveled the Humboldt River
from its beginning to its end and conquered all its obstacles. Here the river
ended and spread its waters to create a vast slough, or marsh, of thousands of
acres. This was a special place and deserves special attention; it was the
convention center for the emigrants.

Some called it the Great Meadows, some the Big Meadows, and others the
Sink. Regardless of what it was called, it was a meeting place, a place for the
emigrants to rest themselves and their animals after 300 miles on the Humboldt
River. Many degrading things were said about the river, but it ended in glory,

its waters spreading out to produce acres of good feed for the animals. Its course lay through the right place in Nevada and now it ended in the right place to help the emigrants through the ordeal that lay ahead - the Forty Mile Desert:

> It would almost seem that these extensive meadows were placed here expressly to supply the means of traversing this desert country. At any rate they are precisely at the point where they are most needed.
>
> Lorenzo Sawyer (1850)

> Here there is grass in abundance, hundreds [of acres] The river here is all scattered over the valley for 3 or 4 miles.
>
> Thomas Christy (1850)

> We arrived at the sink of the river. It empties out on the desert, forming a great marsh or meadow of coarse grass, that covers more than a thousand acres. In many places the grass was higher than a man's head.
>
> G. W. Thissell (1849)

> We cut grass - the best salt grass I ever saw - it is a branchy kind of grass from 4 inches to 14 inches high as thick as hair on a Dogs back.
>
> Thomas Turnbull (1852)

If the stock were turned loose at the Great Meadows, they wandered out in the slough. It was difficult to find them and some became stuck in the mud, so many of the emigrants would wade out and cut the grass:

> There is an abundance of grass at this point for all the stock that can ever reach here. We have to wade to get it, then cart it to the channel, and boat it across that in a wagon box . . . . Two miles below our camp are some falls in the river, at which point the meadows terminate.
>
> Eleazer Stillman Ingalls (1850)

> This marsh for three miles is certainly the liveliest place that one could witness in a lifetime. There is some two hundred and fifty wagons here all the time. Trains going out & others coming in & taking their places, is the constant order of the day.
>
> Vincent Geiger (1849)

Soon trading posts were established here for those who could pay exorbitant prices. It was a place of happiness and also sadness. Some men returned from California with the expectation of meeting their wives or relatives here:

> *A man with his wife came into camp last night on foot, packing what little property they had left on a single ox, the sole remaining animal of their team; but I was informed of a worse case than this by some packers, who said they passed a man and his wife about 11 miles back who were on foot, toiling through the hot sand, the man carrying the blankets and other necessaries, and his wife carrying their only child in her arms, having lost all their team.*
>
> Eleazer Stillman Ingalls (1850)

> *We had thought that some of our profane men were bad enough but the cals are so much worse that we will not compare them. A man here that had came out to meet his wife & she was married to another man before she got here he says that he shall shoot her father before morning.*
>
> Mary Stuart Bailey (1852)

> *Last evening we were called upon to sit with a lady in camp who was not expected to live until morning, we made haste to her camp but when we reached it she had just breathed her last she was a Mrs. Grigsby from Mo who had started in co with a brother in law to join her husband in California her husband who apprised of her coming came out and met her here but oh that meeting he had heard of his sisters death his only sister and felt as if the blow was hard but he had come on to feel a sader his wife did not know him until a short time before she expired when on being asked if she recognized her husband she grew restless puting her arms around his neck while large tears rolled down her cheek she could not speak. Thus they met and thus they parted he was nearly distracted and his voice could be heard full a mile.*
>
> Caroline Richardson (1852)

This area was also an important place for the Indians. The sloughs were filled with ducks, geese, and all kinds of birds, and here the Indians gathered seeds, fish, and anything else they could use for their winter food supply. These were not the Digger Indians that inhabited the Humboldt River, but Paiutes:

More daring and bold Indians seldom or ever have
I seen.

Peter Skene Ogden (1829)

Large number of Pah-Ute Indians gathering the seed of
a large plant which grew in great abundance around the
marsh. The seeds are ground with a stone rolling pin
on a broad stone having the upper surface neatly dressed
into a deep curve. The meal is mixed with water and
moulded into cakes and baked on a bed of coals, made of
dry sage roots which the squaws brought in large cone
shaped baskets . . . . We noticed this morning that
the Indians were busily engaged in making sugar from
wild sugarcane which grew here in abundance. The cane
was cut, and laid in the sun to dry, the juice forming
a crust on the surface. It was then laid on a mat, the
sugar crustation thrashed off, and taken up ready for
use. Stripping some of the sugar from the cane, I
found it had a very pleasant taste, but the canes were
so infested with insects that it was almost impossible
to obtain any pure sugar. That which had been collected
contained a large proportion of insects, but the Indians
gave me to understand that they were sweet, too. However
I had no desire to taste them.

John Steele (1850)

They subsist upon grass-seed, frogs, fish &c - Fish,
however, are very scarce - their manner of catching
which, is somewhat novel and singular. They take the
leg-bone of a sandhill crane, which is generally about
18 inches long, this is fastened in the end of a pole -
they then, by means of a raft made of rushes, which
are very plenty - float along the surface of these
lakes, and spear fish. They exhibit great dexterity
with this simple structure - sometimes killing a fish
with it at a great distance . . .

These lakes are all joined together by means of the
river which passes from one to another, until it reaches
the largest, which has no out-let. The water in this
lake becomes stagnant and very disagreeable - its
surface being covered with a green substance, similar
to a stagnant frog pond. In warm weather there is a
fly, about the size and similar to a grain of wheat,
on this lake, in great numbers. When the wind rolls
the water onto shore, these flies are left on the beach -
the female Indians then carefully gather them into
baskets made of willow branches, and lay them exposed
to the sun until they become perfectly dry, when they
are laid away for winter provender. These flies,
together with grass seed, and a few rabbits, is their
principal food during the winter season.

Zenas Leonard (1833-1834)

> *Many Indians visited us. They are the most intelligent*
> *and best clad we have seen. Some have been in*
> *California diggings, hence their superiority . . . .*
> *They call themselves Piutes.*
>
> > John Edwin Banks (1849)

Some of them were not so well clad:

> *I gave one fellow a pair of pantaloons as, I thought*
> *it would make his company less unacceptable to the*
> *ladies of our camp.*
>
> > Thomas Cramer (1859)

But "stove pipe" hats must have been prized possessions for the Indians:

> *The Indian, doubtless wishing to create a favorable*
> *impression upon the emigrants, had dressed himself*
> *for the occasion. And what do you suppose his toilet*
> *consisted of? One of the old fashion silk stove-pipe*
> *hats, his native modesty and a broad smile. Nothing*
> *else! No breech-clout marred his manly beauty or*
> *detracted from his Adam-like appearance. Of course,*
> *the women looked the other way, while we youngsters*
> *yelled with delight.*
>
> > Velina A. Williams (1853)

> *Just as we were packing to leave, while the sun was*
> *about half an hour high, on looking across the meadows*
> *we saw a stalwart fellow stalking toward us and in the*
> *rays of the setting sun he seemed about seven or eight*
> *feet high. He had on a white fur or silk hat, with a*
> *red string tied about the middle of it, from the brim*
> *of the crown, and not another rag of any kind. He*
> *walked like a monarch and striding into camp, he asked*
> *for bread and we told him could not get any for him,*
> *it was packed up. He then asked for whiskey, and we*
> *told him we had not any in camp, as we had not. The*
> *Indian looked at us for a moment rather scornfully,*
> *and said, "White man lie, God Damn," and turned on*
> *his heel and stalked off across the prairie.*
>
> > David Jackson Staples (1849)

The "Sink" was very important to the emigrants, as they had heard about it long before they reached the Lovelock area, but they were somewhat confused as to what and where it was. Historians today still argue as to its location:

> *Any one who went to California by this overland route*
> *in the early days, and conversed with another of like*
> *experience, was sure to hear again and again of the*
> *Humboldt, the Sink and the desert.*
>
> > Charles D. Ferguson (1850)

> *"How far to the Sink?" has been a question often
> asked, & often answered, and often heard in the
> last month.*
>
> Vincent Geiger (1849)

> *The Sink, about which I have heard as much said,
> the last five or six days, as about a Presidential
> Election.*
>
> Dr. J. S. Shepherd (1850)

> *We are now approaching the Sink, a place looked for
> by emigrants with great anxiety, yet so indefinitely
> described as to make it uncertain whether the
> traveler will recognize it when he reaches it.*
>
> Lorenzo Sawyer (1850)

The emigrants used the word sink to mean different locations in this area,
depending on their own logic as to where the river sinks, their conversations
with others, or their guide books, which varied just as much and only added to
the confusion.

The area near Lovelock where the Humboldt River ends and spreads out
to form the Great Meadows, to the beginning of the Forty Mile Desert is a
distance of fifteen to twenty-five miles. Within this area, different emigrants at
different times might speak of any particular location as the "Sink," or they
might refer to the whole area as the "Sink":

> *There is considerable dispute among Emigrants as to
> what the sink is, and also a difference in various
> guide books on the same subject making distance to
> the Hot Springs and Salmon Trout vary from 4 to 10
> miles according as they date from one or another of
> the ponds, marshes & c of the region.*
>
> Elisha D. Perkins (1849)

> *Still, the name, "Sink of Mary's" or "Humboldt River"
> was applied in our guide book, as well as in
> conversations at Salt Lake City, to the southern or
> lower end of Humboldt Lake, a point some 10 miles
> farther on our way, where, we were told, there were
> several holes dug, close to road. Having always
> understood it to be thus applied, it of course never
> came into our minds to suppose, that our Morman
> friend, when he so particularly marked in the sand
> "the Sink of Mary's" meant the point where at that
> time the water actually disappeared.*
>
> Sara Royce (1849)

We are camped on small byo runing out of the Lake
Mary, or what is more commonly called the sink of
the Humboldt.

Richard O. Hickman (1852)

We came to a narrow slough connecting the lakes
with a large marsh, or as it is generally called
the Lower Sink.

John Steele (1850)

The word "Sink" was still being used in later years to designate the Lovelock area, and today the word is used by different people to mean different places:

The first name of a political nature given the area
(Lovelock) was really "Sink of the Humboldt" at a
convention in Genoa.

Don M. Chase

Humboldt Lake in a wet year - dike is in the background.

When the emigrants left the Great Meadows, their next stop was the "dike," where they prepared to cross the Forty Mile Desert. The distance from the meadows to the dike was fifteen to twenty-five miles, depending on where they had camped.

134

In wet years the waters from the Humboldt River collected from the Great Meadows and flowed further south, to form a lake that most of the emigrants called Humboldt Lake. This lake was between the Great Meadows and the natural earthen dike.

The emigrants had a choice of two roads around the lake, one on the west side and the other on the east side. Most of them took what is generally called the west road, as it was a good road and much smoother:

> *Road from Great Meadows to sink is best we have*
> *traveled in some time - distance 25 miles.*
> John Steele (1850)

Emigrant trail after leaving Great Meadows.

The west road took a southwesterly direction from the Great Meadows and met the trail that went by the point of the mountains in a direct route to the desert:

> *The road goes direct across to strike the old road*
> *some 5 miles. It was a new one, and made through*
> *sage bushes & of course was not very good, but the*
> *old road was as smooth as a table and hard as a*
> *rock. It passed over what is in high water part*
> *of the sink and consequently there was no vegetation*

save a few sage bushes, which were upon mounds
several feet above the level . . . Twelve miles
upon the old road brought us to the sink, the
disideration of long hoped for weeks.
                                  Vincent Geiger (1849)

Humboldt Lake varied in size with each description. The size depended on the year; some years were very wet:

We are now at the end of our Journey of the Humboldt
River, here she sinks beneath the sands of the great
desert, but before she is lost in sight forever, her
waters spread out into a lake some six or eight miles
in length by one and a half in breadth.
                                  John Hawkins Clark (1852)

In two miles came to the west lake of the sink, along
which we traveled 10 miles on Lake toward southwest.
                                  John Steele (1850)

A fine sheet of clear water, perhaps fifteen miles
in length forty in circumference.
                                  Horace Greeley (1859)

Lake 5 miles long 1½ miles wide.
                                  Madison B. Moorman (1850)

There was found a mud lake 10 miles long and four or
five miles wide, a veritable sea of slime, "a slough
of despond," an ocean of ooze, a bottomless bed of
alkaline poison, which emitted a nauseous odor and
presented the appearance of utter desolation.
                                  Reuben Cole Shaw (1849)

In dry years, Humboldt Lake was described differently:

Nearly the whole of our days travel 20 miles today
and a part of yesterday was evidently under water
but a few years since now at this time Marys [Humboldt]
river sinks and disappears intirely some 8 or 10 miles
above the small shallow pond known as Ogdens Lake and
this whole region is now intirely dried up and has the
most thirsty appearance of any place I ever witnessed.
                                  James Clyman (1846)

On some maps a lake is indicated at the lower end of
the Humboldt River we could see nothing of such a
lake, However one could tell that the barren, salty,
low area must be covered with water at certain seasons;
then this wide basin must have the appearance of a
rather large lake.
                                  Heinrich Lienhard (1846)

*There is nothing of the appearance of a Lake about
it, as you can only see the water about in spots.
It therefore has more the appearance of Pond than a
lake. Takeing it all in all, it is one of the most
disagreable and loathsome looking places on the face
of the earth.*

James A. Pritchard (1849)

The lake and the surrounding ponds were a haven for the ducks, geese,
and other waterfowl, but mud prevented the emigrants from using the waterfowl
to replenish their food supply:

*The ponds of the sink were covered with all kinds of
wild fowl, geese, ducks, curlews, snipes, cranes, &c.
Perfectly secure from man or beast, as the ground is
a perfect mire in every direction. Continuing around
the sink or marsh, in a South East course you come to
the "last wells" at the foot of the marsh & ponds,
being the last place where water can be obtained before
crossing the desert to Salmon Trout [Truckee River] . . . .
While we were encamped at the last wells, after dark,
one of our party fired a gun heavily loaded in the
direction of the Lake which was only some 100 yards
from us, & the noise made by the wings of the frightened
birds was like thunder, & we could hear it continuing
up the plain as flock after flock take the alarm like
the rumbling of thunder after the first heavy roll.*

Elisha D. Perkins (1849)

The water in the lake at this lower end was not good to use:

*One can get an idea of how it tastes by making a
strong solution of tepid water and bitter salts and
adding several rotton eggs. Such a mixture would
produce about the same effect on the human body as
would the water of the sink. Only dire thirst and
the knowledge that one would have to walk forty
miles before coming to real water could force
anyone to take a drink of this diabolic liquid.*

Heinrich Lienhard (1846)

*Where we encamped we found it necessary to dig wells
for water. These wells, about four feet in diameter
and of a trifle less depth, furnished us abundant
supply of water, but intensely brackish, bitter with
salt and sulphur.*

William G. Johnston (1849)

At the lower end of the lake a slough ran out and disappeared between
"two hills," as stated in some diaries. These two hills were probably the low

place in the dike where the lake broke through in later years. Byron McKinstry traveled down the east side of the lake, and made this comment at the end near the dike:

> There was a slough that continued on from the lower
> end of the lake, passing between the hills, some
> 20 or 30 ft. wide, no current to it. The cattle
> would not drink it. I am told that there is a well
> on the other side of the slough which is drinkable,
> though impregnated with sulphur. This slough runs
> between two small hills & here is a ford. The road
> that comes down on the other side of the river comes
> in here and as we intended to take the Truckey route
> I suppose that we should have crossed to the other
> side. But we were told that the Truckey route took
> off to the right four miles from here.

The two roads that went down both sides of the lake from the Great Meadows joined near the dike:

> North and south roads came together at end of Sink.
>   Thomas Turnbull (1852)

Now the name "Sink" is used for the area at the end of Humboldt Lake where there is a natural dam. This dam was formed by the wave action of ancient Lake Lahontan, the great inland lake which once filled this section of Nevada. The obstruction, in back of which Humboldt Lake formed, is considered the starting place for the Forty Mile Deserts. It is now called the Dike or Natural Dike, although some maps call it the Humboldt Bar:

> At dusk we reached what is properly the Sink. An
> embankment some twenty feet high extends across the
> bed of the river, extending from mountain to mountain,
> perhaps one and a half miles wide . . . The barrier
> has all the regularity of art, and what is remarkably
> strange, it has a large slough on the opposite side.
>   John Edwin Banks (1849)

> Crossing a low ridge and descending on West side to
> the marsh at noon we stopped and pulled some rushes
> which oxen eagerly devoured.
>   John Steele (1850)

> We made a drive of 20 miles today, passing the sink,
> and camping over a low bluff upon the bank of a slough
> coming from the southwest quite close to two trading
> posts.
>   Dr. John H. Wayman (1852)

At the border of this desert lake, a few feet higher
than the water is a plateau of sand, covered with
sage brush and stones. We were there in the last
week of August. Fresh water was not to be had
except at a place a half mile from our camp, where
there was a seepage spring . . . Not far from the
spring was situated a rude shack, known as "Black's
Trading Post."

William A. Maxwell (1857)

Black's was the trading post where a man by the name of Tooly was captured and accused of robbing and murdering an emigrant. Jurors were found among the emigrants, a judge appointed, a trial held, and Tooly was found guilty. According to Maxwell, the verdict was harsh: "You can have your choice to be shot or hanged to the uplifted tongue of a wagon." Tooly decided to make a run for it, and was shot, after which everybody went about their business again.

Humboldt Lake had no visible outlet during the early years of the migration. The slough below the dike was formed by seepage, or as some emigrants thought, "a subterranean outlet." They camped and cut grass on both sides of the dike. Preparing for their desert crossing, they filled everything they could with water, even their boots:

Here you prepare for the desert and pass over a small
ridge, to a valley where part of the waters of Mary's
River, having escaped from the Lake sinks.

P. L. Platt (1849-1850)

I had with me a pair of long top leather boots; these
I filled with hay just as full as I could stuff them . . .
At 2 P.M., all being in readiness we saddled up and
adjusting my boots, filled with hay, across my saddle,
one boot on each side, I rode my horse out into the
slough of water and with my tin cup filled each boot
full of water.

Lemuel C. McKeeby (1850)

The Donner party traveled the Humboldt River route from west of Elko, where they had again joined the main trail after taking the Hastings Cutoff. They suffered all the trials and tribulations that the Humboldt Valley could offer, including the anxiety of being the last group on the trail late in the season. By the time they started down the Humboldt they were a disorganized and disheartened group, but they made the trip down the river quickly. There was bickering, quarreling, and one murder, two if you include their leaving an old man in the desert to die. When they came to the sink the Indians stole twenty-one head of cattle that might later have saved their lives. Some of the families had lost everything and were now walking, but they still had to keep plodding and prepare to cross the Forty Mile Desert.

At the dike or just beyond, the emigrants of 1848 and later had to make a decision as to which trail they would take. The Truckee trail, leading to the Truckee River and over Donner Summit, or the one to the Carson River, going over Kit Carson Pass. Either way there were forty miles of desert to cross.

The Truckee route was older. It had been used since 1844, and the desert section was easier because there was not as much sand. Also, half way across there was a hot spring, the water from which could be used by both animals and people when cooled. The emigrants had heard about the Truckee River and the many crossings up the canyon, and later parties had heard the tragic story of the Donner party and the difficult crossing of the Sierra, so most of the gold seekers took the Carson route.

The Carson route was newer. Most of it had been opened in the latter part of 1848, by a group of Mormons returning to Salt Lake City from California. They had traveled east from Placerville over Kit Carson Pass and then down the Carson River, probably leaving the river where Williams and Honey Lake Smiths stations were later built, near the present settlement of Silver Springs. After leaving the Carson River they traveled to the bend of the Truckee River near Wadsworth, and then across the desert by the Truckee trail. This group returning to Salt Lake met Joseph Chiles on the Humboldt River and told him about their new route. When Chiles reached the dike he decided to take it and went directly across the desert to the Carson River. This completed the Carson River route that most of the gold seekers would follow.

There is much current debate as to where these two trails divided. This writer does not intend to enter this argument, but would like to state that there was more than one division point. The emigrants were individualists and did not always follow a set pattern. Sometimes the land was wet and sometimes very dry, which affected their course. This was flat country and trails could easily be changed.

Many of the emigrant diaries were written days, weeks, or in some cases,

MOONLIGHT CAMP SCENE ON THE HUMBOLDT.

David Rohrer Leeper

years after the event occurred. Some say the trail divided even before it reached the dike, others name different places in the desert beyond the dike:

> *We at last got to the end of the lake & to the forks of the road; the left hand prong crossed the desert to Carson River & the right across the desert to Trucke River.*
>
> James Pressley Yager (1863)

> *3 miles from the sink the road leaves the old road which passes by the Hot Springs and goes to the left. In a few miles we came to an alkali spring around which were several dead oxen.*
>
> Charles Gould (1849)

> *Road passes around the lake, keeping near it, and the long sloughs beyond it, twenty miles, where the road forks - the road leading to the right is the Truckee Road, and the other the Carson.*
>
> Andrew Child (1850)

> *A few miles out we crossed small stream, excessively salt and utterly unfit to drink. Here the trail forked, the road to the right leading to the northern pass of the Sierra Nevada, via Truckee River; while the other, a newer route led to Carson River, and a more southerly pass.*
>
> William G. Johnston (1849)

Where was the sink? Where was the division of the trails? Where were many things that we read about in these diaries and have difficulty reconciling with what we find now? One modern writer put it well:

> *The golden army of 1850 will find a new California Trail and mention points of which the Argonauts of 1849 never heard. We ourselves, even, are confused by the multitude of memories and cannot agree as to where certain incidents occurred or when. As each one become more conformed, through the years, of the correctness of his own view, who will ever reconcile the discrepancies.*
>
> Archer B. Hulbert

The emigrants had now conquered the Humboldt River, had experienced the sink, and were ready for the third challenge of crossing Nevada - the desert. Crossing the desert was not so bad in itself; it was the conditions under which the emigrants labored that made for the many hardships. The long pull of three hundred miles down the Humboldt River with poor water and feed left the animals in a weakened conditon, and the emigrants themselves in a like situation. It was near the end of the journey. Four months or more had already been spent on the road, and now this desert had to be crossed:

> *It would not be as bad as it is, did it not follow close after the Humboldt River, the water of which has such a weakening influence on the stock, that it is next to a miracle to get over safe without leaving some, if not all of them behind.*
> Dr. J. S. Shepherd (1850)

> *All are preparing and dreading to cross, by far the worst desert we have met yet. They, perhaps, would not mind it, and neither would I, if we had plenty to eat; but here are hundreds already lamenting their anticipated death, and suffering on the burning plain. Expect to find the worst desert you ever saw and then find it worse than you expected.*
> John Wood (1850)

> *The passage of this desert would be no hard matter to old and experienced travelers well fixed, but to the untutored pilgrim, with worn out teams, poor feed and bad water, it is a matter of some importance.*
> John Hawkins Clark (1852)

Generally speaking, the emigrants tried to start into the desert in the late afternoon and travel all night so as to avoid the worst heat:

> *As it takes 24 hours to cross the desert, it was thought best to start in the evening, so we left camp an hour before sun down.*
> Helen McCowen Carpenter (1856)

> *As does everyone else we shall travel by night, the want of water being much less felt by both animals & men.*
> Arthur M. Menefee (1857)

As they prepared for their desert ordeal, the emigrants were approximately twenty to twenty-five miles southwest of Lovelock, to the east of Highway 80.

VIII. The Truckee River Route

The distance from the dike to the Truckee River is forty miles. This is the Forty Mile Desert on the Truckee Route; since it is the older of the two deserts bearing this name its crossing will be examined first.

The emigrants' first objective was to reach "Boiling Springs," a distance of twenty miles:

> *We turn to the right and move on to the Desert. The*
> *road passes over a rolling and rather rough country*
> *for twenty miles to Boiling Springs.*
> Andrew Child (1850)

Emigrant trail nearing Boiling Springs.

The first section of the desert trail was good and level, then it left the plains and salt flats and gradually climbed to higher ground:

The road now went in a more westerly direction, whereas
in the last three or four days we had been traveling
almost due south. At first we drove through low country,
but gradually we climbed considerably higher . . . .
The rocks had a peculiar formation, such as I had never
saw before or since.

Heinrich Lienhard (1846)

Peculiar rock formation.

The emigrants arrived at the hot springs about midnight. These springs are now called Brady's Hot Springs, but they no longer look the way the emigrants saw them. They are located half-way across this forty-mile stretch and made a good resting place. The water was not good, but when cooled it could be used by both animals and humans:

At moonset we came to the Boiling Well where the ground
shoots steam like the mouth of Hell.

Jo Utter (1847)

The water is as hot as boiling water can be made. A
thick steam is constantly rolling from this boiler of
nature. The water is a little brackish but answers

*very well for all purposes for man and beast when
cooled.*

Cyrus C. Loveland (1850)

Remains of the Boiling Hot Springs.

*The water is clear and the springs deep. The temperature
of the water was about 210 degrees . . . The water is
impregnated with common salt, but not so much as to
render it unfit for cooking purposes, and by taking a
portion from the spring and adding a sufficient
quantity of tea, it is as good as if it was boiled
over fire. At one place the boiling water spouts up
from 8 to 10 feet.*

Richard O. Hickman (1852)

*The country around these springs is uneven, and barren,
truly a desert place. The springs are on the side of
a low, rocky ridge. That which seems to be the
fountain head is a chasm in a ledge from which the
boiling water rises at intervals in a column about
two feet in diameter to the height of fifteen feet,
emitting clouds of roaring steam.*

John Steele (1850)

Dike to Boiling Springs

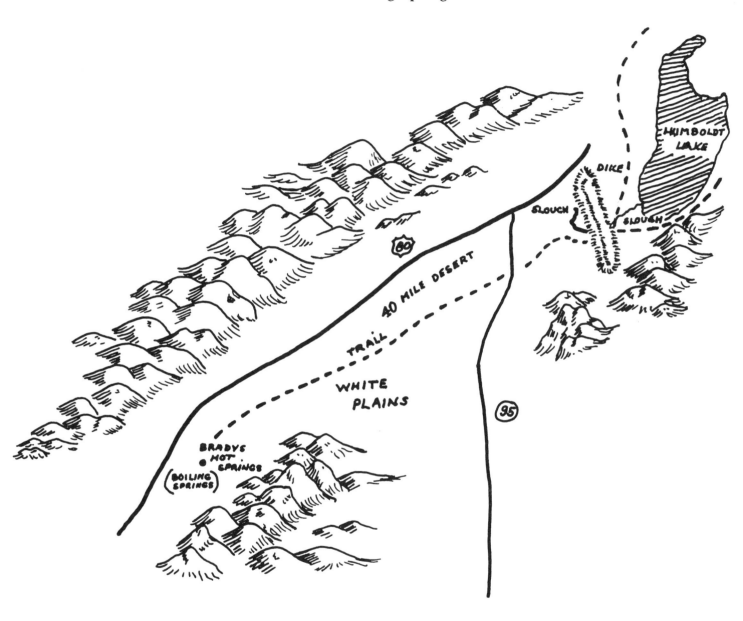

This route was opened in 1844 by the Murphy-Townsend-Stevens Party. Those taking this route were heading for the Truckee River through Reno and over Donner Summit.

From the Dike to the River is 40 miles; this is the 40-mile desert on the Truckee River Route. It is over barren ground and alkali flats.

147

The emigrants continually had to lighten the loads in their wagons, and these springs received their share of the abandoned property.

There were many foreigners on the trail, especially Germans. They expressed themselves well in their diaries, even if their spelling was not quite standard:

> *Theas springs are the greatest curorisityes i ever*
> *saw thear is over a hundred of them all of them*
> *boiling hot one of them is very large one another one*
> *boiles up in a hole about two feet over at stated*
> *times it dies entirely away and then in a moment it*
> *sprouts up two feet and throws the boiling water for*
> *ten feet around the property that lays scattered around*
> *here is increadable thear is over a dozen good wagons*
> *and by the old irons laying around at least as many*
> *more had been burnt up log chains cooking utencils*
> *and in fact everything that one can think of amonst*
> *other things i noticed a splend[ed] turning lathe*
> *it could not have cost less than one hundred and*
> *fifty dollars we counted fifty four dead oxen between*
> *hear and the sulphur wells.*
>
>   Elizabeth Page (1849)

Boiling Springs was also a place of tragedy:

> *Susan Westfall fell in one of these springs & got*
> *badly scalded. At these springs is the greatest*
> *reck of wagons and carriages that my eye ever beheld -*
> *We made tea & coffee out of these springs which drank*
> *very well.*
>
>   Arthur M. Menefee (1857)

> *We visited the boiling springs, which are, indeed a*
> *great curiosity, with their waters foaming and gurgling,*
> *the noise of which at times, they tell me, may be heard*
> *at a half mile's distance. In one of them we saw the*
> *bones of a man who, being deranged, threw himself into*
> *it a year or two since, and immediately perished. A*
> *women and a child were also killed by falling into it*
> *last summer.*
>
>   Harriet S. Ward (1853)

After resting a few hours, the emigrants started on the remaining twenty miles to the Truckee River. The trail was good until they came to the sand, which put more strain on the weakened animals than most could endure:

> *At sunrise we left the hot springs, and bending around*
> *the base of a gray hill, our trail followed down a*
> *channel that once might have been a watercourse, but*

The Boiling Spring to the Truckee River

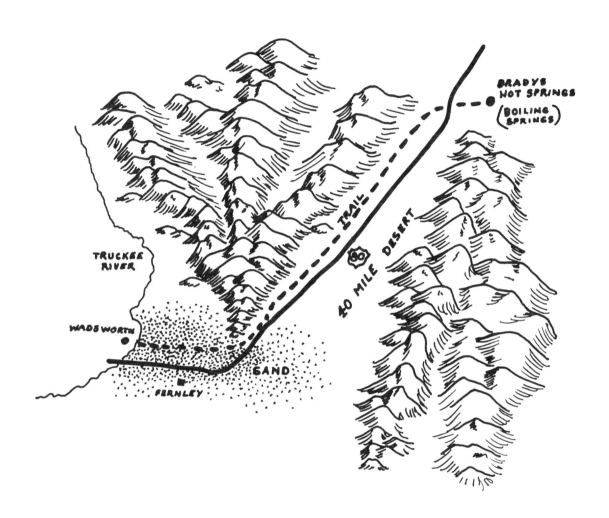

The Boiling Spring is half way to the Truckee River and the water, even when cooled, was not good but it was usable.

Approximately seven miles from the Truckee River the trail entered deep sand which was very difficult for the emigrants to cross.

*was now dry and crusted over with salt. Near this we
found a human body.*
                              John Steele (1850)

*Left here over a very good road, but dusty, until we
came in about 10 miles of the Trucky River, then we
had a pretty hard time to the river reaching the
river soon after light leaving several of the cattle
behind and several lost and died. One or two of the
boys liked to have suffocated for the want of water.
Some of the boys went back & found 41 of the cattle,
carrying water to the poor suffers . . . Have two
in camp not expected to live, Susan Westfall and
Mrs. Britton.*
                              Arthur M. Menefee (1857)

*Very little of note save dust and brightness of the
glittering sand, now and then a grave.*
                              John Clark of Virginia (1852)

Before reaching the river, they had to cross a very difficult sandy stretch that took its toll of many animals. This is the sand east of the modern Nevada Cement Plant, near Fernley.

Many of the emigrants were walking toward the end of their journey and the sand was just as difficult for them as for the animals:

*At noon, came to a sandy hill . . . After ascending
the hill it was typical desert all the rest of the
way. There was deep sand for eight miles, & the
road on both sides was strewn with dead cattle.*
                              Richard O. Hickman (1852)

*We then pushed on till five in the morning when we
came to a heavy sandy hill from this to river a
distance of 8 miles was nothing but sand from 6 to
8 inches deep two of the teams gave out before
they had got one mile we passed thirty wagons
that had taken thear cattel off and drove on to
the river to water them oxen were laying every few
hundred yards.*
                              Elizabeth Page (1849)

*We are now seven miles from the Truckee River, but
the road here becomes very sandy and heavy. After
traveling three miles the teams begin to give out,
so we had to unhitch them from the wagons and send
them on to grass and water.*
                              Eliza Ann McAuley (1852)

150

Beginning of the sand
that extended to the Truckee River.

*About 2 O'clock we struck the heavy sand 10 miles
from Trucky River, & had the utmost difficulty in
getting our stock thro - stopping every few yards
to rest . . . . All along the desert from the very
start, even the waysides was strewed with the dead
bodies of oxen, mules and horses and the stench was
horrible. All our traveling experience furnishes no
parallel to this.*
                                    Bennett C. Clark (1849)

*I was over come and tired out, I would travel a little
and I would lay down on the sand and rest and the sun
shining on me, There is no timber thare I thought I
would never get through and I laide down to kick the
bucket; but I thought of home and it give me a little
more grit and I would get up, and stager along. I
was so thirsty my tonge and lips cracked and bled but
I was able to get to the water and after drinking a
little - I dare not drink much - I felt better.*
                                    Andrew Orvis (1849)

Relief parties were sent out from California to establish relief stations and help
those emigrants in need. The 1850 report of the Waldo relief party describes the

suffering:

> At the lower Truckee Crossing beef had been deposited,
> and a number of stout animals sent to carry sick
> emigrants across the desert. Several starving men
> were encountered, and the dead bodies of others who
> had succumbed. Few were found with provisions save
> their exhausted teams; one fourth, haveing no animals,
> lived on the putrefying carcasses, thus absorbing
> disease. Cholera broke out Sept. 8th, in one small
> train carrying off 8 persons in 3 hours, several
> more being expected to die. From the sink westward
> the havoc was fearful. Of 20,000 emigrants still
> back of the desert fully 15,000 were destitute and
> their greatest suffering was yet to come.
>> Hubert Howe Bancroft

The emigrants came to the river at its bend between Wadsworth and Highway 80. After forty to sixty-five miles with practically no water, and only barely drinkable water for weeks before that, the cold, clear flowing Truckee was a beautiful sight. The emigrants had also not seen a tree for hundreds of miles:

> We beheld the green banks and crystal clear waters of
> the Truckee River by the morning sun; and it was to us
> the River of Life.
>> Elisha Brooks (1852)

> The Salmon Trout being lined with the finest cotton
> woods I ever saw. No one can imagine how delightful
> the sight of a tree is after such long stretches of
> desert, until they have tried it, we have seen very
> few of any kind since leaving the Platt, & what a
> luxury after our mules were taken care of, to lay
> down in their shade & make up our two nights loss
> of sleep, & hear the wind rustling their leaves &
> whistling among their branches.
>> Elisha D. Perkins (1849)

Here, as in the Lovelock area, the emigrants encountered Paiute Indians:

> There are great numbers of Indians about here. They
> call themselves Piutes. They are very friendly and
> more intelligent than the Root Diggers. They procured
> for me great numbers of little fish resembling a
> sardine which they caught with ingenious little hooks
> made of a little stick one forth of an inch in length
> to which was fastened nearly at right angles, a little
> thorn. These they baited with the outside of an insect.
> The line was simply a linen thread with six of these
> little hooks attached.
>> Mariett Foster Cummings (1852)

[The Youth's Companion]

Bend of the Truckee River near Wadsworth
where the emigrants had their first good
water and saw trees for the first time in months.

After leaving this resting place the trail wound up the Truckee River for thirty miles to the Truckee Meadows, where Reno is now located. This section was very difficult because of the narrow canyon, the swift current, and the rocks in the river, making the crossings strenuous and irritating to the emigrants. Most of them followed close to the river, but there were detours in the mountains to avoid these crossings. Some reported fording the river as many as thirty-eight times, others only a few.

> It has been usual to ford the river twenty or thirty
> times within as many miles, to avoid the walls of
> rock. The fords are all very bad, the river being
> a rapid stream, and its bottom covered with large
> rocks. By following the mountain road, all of these
> fords but eight (8) may be avoided.
>   Andrew Child (1850)

Truckee River near Wadsworth to Truckee Meadows

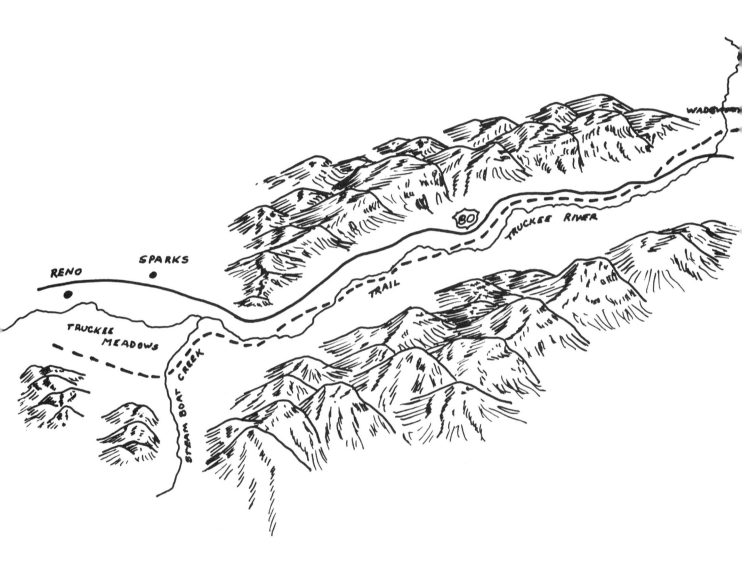

The water is now good and there is feed for the animals. The banks of the
river are lined with shade trees.

The river is not a wide stream but it generally flows fast. Some sections have
slippery rocks which made fording the stream difficult. The river flows
through a canyon which necessitated many river crossings.

*We soon begin to cross and recross the darndest rough
and rocky fords ever attempted before. The water
swift, deep and full of round boulders from the size
of a dinner pot to that of a 4 foot stump.*
John Clark of Virginia (1852)

*After a week of painful traveling we came to the
Truckee, which we had to cross thirty-eight times
before we arrived at the base of the eastern slope
of the Sierra Nevada.*
Nicholas Carriger (1846)

*A pleasant walk this morn brought us to the third and
last crossing of the Truckee, which is very good. . . . . .
At one time today we found ourselves upon the banks
of the Truckee with a narrow, rough, rocky path,
barely wide enough for the wagons to cross over,
and the craggy, rocky mountains rising four hundred
feet immediately above our heads.*
Harriet S. Ward (1853)

Trail along the Truckee River between Wadsworth and Reno.

The many crossings of the Truckee made it very difficult for the emigrants; but some also thought of it as a beautiful stream, and one diarist observed the large trout that used to run up it from Pyramid Lake. It was for these trout that Fremont first named the river Salmon Trout:

> *Salmon Trout is a most beautiful stream, rushing &*
> *roaring over the rocks & its stony bed like a New*
> *England mountain river & the waters as clear as*
> *crystal . . .*
>
> *Saw in our course along the banks of the stream,*
> *numbers of those beautiful fish from which the river*
> *takes it name; but had no time to spend in catching*
> *them, indeed others who had tried it say they will*
> *not bite at this season of the year. Some of these*
> *fish were two feet long, beautifully spotted like*
> *the New England trout.*
>
> Elisha D. Perkins (1849)

The trail entered the Truckee Meadows at the point where the Reno-Sparks sewer plant is now located. Shortly after passing this point the emigrants encountered Steamboat Creek, which they called a slough. This creek has very steep banks and is muddy, but some enterprising emigrants crossed by constructing a willow bridge:

> *We have crossed a slough, the crossing of which was*
> *fixed and bridged by our Captain & party ahead.*
> *Before this was done, it is said it was almost*
> *impassable, each having to be cordelled across.*
> *We passed over it safely & encamped in this lovely*
> *valley, with blue grass to the horses' knees.*
>
> Vincent Geiger (1849)

> *This is a beautiful valley about ten miles wide,*
> *bounded on all sides with high and rugged mountains,*
> *some of which are heavily timbered. About half of*
> *this valley is thickly covered with grass, the other*
> *half perfectly barren. On the east side is a slough,*
> *by crossing this it is said to cut off six miles . . .*
> *Repaired the Willow Bridge, crossed and took cut off.*
>
> Cyrus C. Loveland (1850)

The slough also took its toll, however:

> *We came out of the canon into a broad noble valley*
> *walled on all sides by lofty moun[tains] and covered*
> *with a luxurant coat of grass we had a muddy slough*
> *to cross to get to camp thear was a man killed in*
> *it yesterday he was crossing on a mule when the mule*

fell down and rolled on him and mashed him in the
mud so that he died before they could get him out.
Elizabeth Page (1849)

Slough near Reno that the emigrants
had a difficult time crossing.

The majority of the emigrants did not attempt to cross the slough where they first came to it. Instead, they went south for about two miles, past the present Hidden Valley Golf Course, to an easier crossing. Then they turned west along the base of Rattlesnake Mountain:

> *At 4 P.M. we emerged from the Canon into what is*
> *called Mist Valley, a beautiful level plain covered*
> *with fine grass, some 10 miles across & formed by*
> *the widening of the mountain ranges. Through this*
> *valley the river winds after leaving the gorge on*
> *the other side, its course marked by a line of*
> *cotton woods & willows. Soon after entering the*
> *valley we took a trail leaving the road to the*
> *right & supposing to be a "Cutoff" as the road*
> *wound around a belt of marsh which crosses the*
> *valley at right angles to the river. We followed*

*this trail around the base of the hills & soon found
ourselves going off quite in contrary direction to
the course of the road, & the marsh on our right was
entirely uncrossable a perfect quagmire . . .*

*The view from our present camp is grand. In front
of us towers a range of the loftiest mountains we
have yet seen their tops covered with perpetual snow
and some places covered on their sides.*
Elisha D. Perkins (1849)

Emigrant trail south of the Hidden Valley Golf Course.

The well-known diarist, James Clyman, described the slough and the
detour to the south when he was going east from California:

> *We came to a deep muddy brook running through a handsome
> prarie valley went up the brook about 3 miles before we
> found a crossing passed down along side of a steep
> volcanick mountain, shewing immence quantities of rough
> slagg and other vitrified matter.*

After crossing the slough the trail continued west near the Reno–Sparks
Convention Center, through the Washoe County Golf Course, and up Plumb Lane

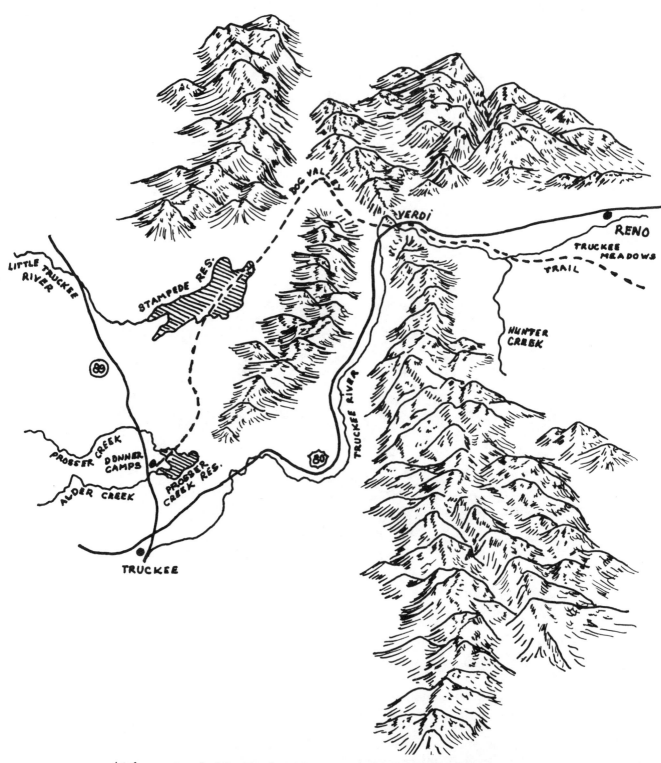

At the west end of the Truckee Meadows near Verdi, the trail leaves the
Truckee River to enter the mountains. It goes up Dog Valley Grade, down
Hoke Valley and southwest to Alder Creek. The two Donner families camped
at Alder Creek; this was the end of the journey for many of them.

to the crossing of the Truckee River at the Mayberry Bridge:

> *After dinner drove two miles and crossed 9th time*
> *above a spring branch.*
>
> Cyrus C. Loveland (1850)

The emigrants forded the Truckee at a spring branch (Hunter Creek), then headed toward Verdi and past it to the Dog Valley grade. Here they left the river to avoid the canyon from Verdi to the town of Truckee. This Dog Valley section was opened in 1845 by the eighty-year-old mountain man and guide, Caleb Greenwood:

> *Here we left Truckee River and ascended the mountain,*
> *through thick forest, across difficult, rocky mountain*
> *slope. We were in constant fear that the wheels of*
> *our wagon would strike against the giant firs on the*
> *lower side of the road.*
>
> Heinrich Lienhard (1846)

At the top of the Dog Valley grade the emigrants descended a steep hill into Dog Valley. After a short rest they left the valley by an easy ascent on the south end.

The trail descended this steep hill into Dog Valley
and then ascended an easy incline out at left of picture.

> *Then descended to a little valley, grass and cold*
> *spring branch. Nooned here, distance from the river*
> *five miles. After dinner ascended gradual rise of*
> *two miles to the top of the ridge where we made for*
> *the firs and a peep at the snowy mountains.*
>
> Cyrus C. Loveland (1850)

Stampede and Prosser Dams and many logging roads make it difficult now to follow the trail in this area. After the emigrants came out of Dog Valley they descended to the Little Truckee River (Wind River), crossed it, and traveled without any trouble to Prosser Creek (John's Creek) and Alder Creek. The trail was probably either on or close to the old Dog Valley road from Reno to Truckee:

> *It is 9 miles to Wind River from the spring branch*
> *where we camped, 9 miles from Wind River to John's*
> *River, & 6 miles from John's River to the waters of*
> *Truckeys River.*
>
> Jacob R. Snyder (1845)

The trail that is accepted by most historians goes up Alder Creek, through the Tahoe Donner development, and then down by Truckee High School toward Donner Lake. However, this writer believes that, after 1845, most of the emigrants did not go up Alder Creek but took instead the shorter, more direct, and easier route to the present town of Truckee and the Truckee River. They then moved on toward Donner Lake. The present Highway 89 between Truckee and Alder Creek is very close to this trail. In his notes on the Nicholas Carriger diary, Dale Morgan describes this route:

> *Left Prosser Creek and its tributary Alder Creek and*
> *crossed a small hill to reach Donner Creek about*
> *where it enters to Truckee near present Truckee.*

Writing later about the town of Truckee, Nona McGlashen states:

> *Parallel to the town ran the old emigrant road along*
> *which the merchants continued to build (This is now*
> *Commercial Row).*

Other accounts confirm this theory:

> *The road still the same, except a little rougher.*
> *Four miles, the road turned left. Here, upon our*
> *left, distant some hundred yards from the road was*
> *Truckee River in all its glory again, splashing and*

Alder Creek to the Summit of the Sierra Nevada

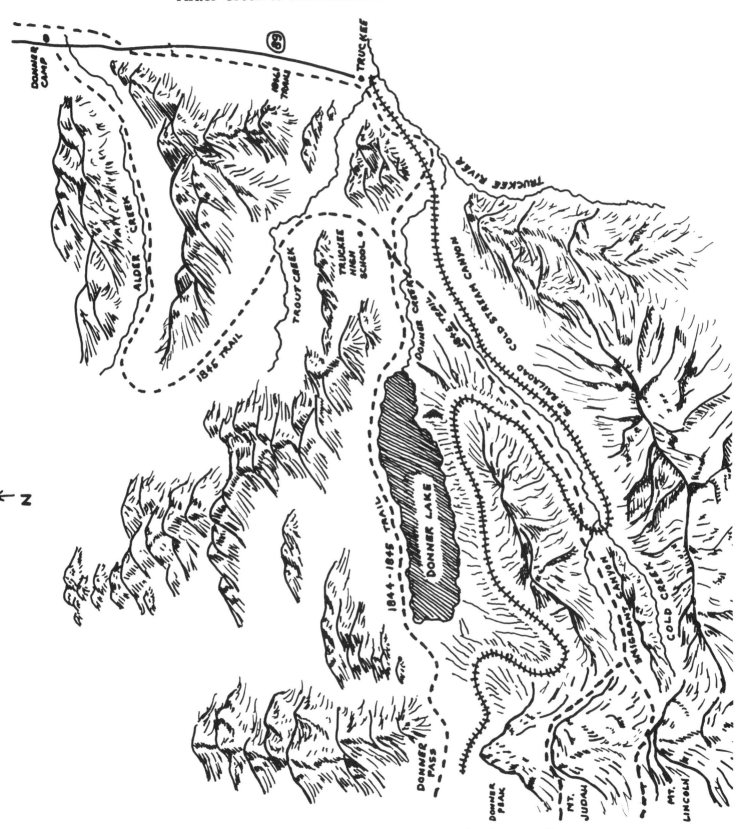

The first trail was along the north side of Donner Lake but later a trail was
opened up through Cold Stream Canyon to Emigrant Canyon.

dashing over the rocks.

Vincent Geiger (1849)

*By keeping the Bald Mountain on the left and pursuing
the most eligible route, Truckeys River cannot be
missed. We struck Truckeys River & encamped about
1 mile from the point where we struck it. Near the
point where we struck it are 2 large isolated rocks in
the valley . . . Packed this morning at 8 o'clock
and followed the river on the right side until we
struck a lake at the foot of the declivity of the
Back Bone of the California Mountains. This Lake is
3 miles long & from 1 to 1½ miles wide. We passed a
log cabin built by the Emigrants of last year.*

Jacob R. Snyder (1845)

Jacob Snyder was traveling in the year 1845, and the cabin that he saw was the one built by Moses Schallenbarger and his two companions, who stayed at the lake to guard the wagons left by the Murphy-Townsend-Stevens party in 1844. The next year some members of the Donner party used this cabin and built two more. Some of the emigrants confused Donner Creek with the Truckee River. They did not see the junction of the two and presumed that the Truckee River started in Donner Lake, or Truckee Lake, as they called it.

The emigrants were now camped near Donner Lake. Cabins noted at this site after 1846 were those used by the Donner party; they were reportedly burned by General Kearny when he returned from California after the war with Mexico. There were three cabins, and apparently they were not completely destroyed, as many later emigrants wrote about them in their diaries:

*Visited Truckee Lake, half a mile above our camp.
Near outlet of Lake were ruins of the cabins built
by ill fated Donner Party. Most of the cabins had
been burned, and their charred remains, and whitened
bones, half buried among withered pine leaves are sad
memories of the event. Also tall stumps, some 20 feet
high, showing the trees were cut, gave an idea of the
great depth of snow.*

John Steele (1850)

*Graves and Fosters Cabins are the only ones that are
standing yet and they present a gloomy appearance. In
Fosters there were the clothes which were worn by
females and also long female hair which appeared as
if it had fallen from the head and any quantity of
bones in and around the cabins.*

John A. Markle (1849)

*We were informed that the cabins of the "Lamentable
Donner Party" were also on the road, as well as also
[that] the [Pyramid, or Donner] Lake [was] but one
mile from the present trail. I immediately started
off to look for these mournful monuments of human
suffering. One was only 150 yds. from our camp upon
the left of the trail. This [cabin] was still standing.
It was two in one, there being a seperation of logs
between. The timbers were from 8 inches to a foot in
diameter, about 8 or 9 ft. high & covered over with
logs upon which had been placed branches & limbs of
trees, dirt &c. The logs were fitted very nicely
together, there being scarcely a crevice between.
There was one door to each, entering from the north
and from the road.*

*There were piles of bones around but mostly of cattle,
although I did find some half dozen human ones of
different parts. Just to the left of these was a few
old burnt logs, which evidently had been one of those
[cabins] which had been burnt. Here was nearly the
whole of a skeleton. Several small stockings were
found which still contained the bones of the leg &
foot. Remnants of old clothes, with pieces of boxes,
stockings & bones in particular, was all that was left
to mark that it had once been inhabited.*

*In the centre of each was a hole dug which had either
served as a fireplace or to bury their dead. The trees
around were cut off 10 ft. from the ground, showing the
immense depth the snow must have been. After examing
this I passed on one mile where the road went to the
left in a more southerly direction. The old trail went
on straight down the valley to the Lake which was
distant one mile . . .*

*In returning I came to another of the cabins, but which
had been burned by order of Gen'l Kearney. Here also
I found many human bones. The skulls had been sawed
open for the purpose, no doubt, of getting out the
brains, & the bones had all been sawed open & broken
to obtain the last particle of nutriment.*
                              Vincent Geiger (1849)

One emigrant spent a very uneasy night on guard duty at this camp:

*We came to the Donner Camp whear the most of them
perished the winter before. they had trimmed the pines
of their limbs for fuel. their camp was in a thick
forrest of pines, not far from doner lake. the snow
was verry deep. we found bones and sculls scattered
about it was a most horrible sight-they had mashed
the bones to get the marrow. some wild indians come*

165

in our camp in the evening to take observations the
wildest looking savages we had seen. they had never
seen a white man before according to their actions by
and by their leader said. wedy. wedy. hoddy. hoddy.
and dissipeared in the dark forrest. I stood guard in
the latter part of the night. And thoudt of all the
ghosts and hobgoblins i could think of or ever herd
of. besides the sculls bones and the dark forest it
was a most dismal place. day come and drove all the
specter away.

> Abner Blackburn (1847)

The Donner party struggled across the Forty Mile Desert, most of them walking and some even carrying small children. One man was murdered by his comrades, but the rest made it to the Truckee River and the Truckee Meadows (Reno). Here was good grass and water, but again they lingered too long. On his return from Sutter's Fort, Charles Stanton found the Donners on the Truckee River. One of two men who had left the party in eastern Nevada to go ahead for help, he arrived with seven mules packed with dried beef and other supplies. The other man, William McCutchen, was too sick to return.

It was now the end of October, and the group was facing mountains covered with snow. No one in the party was keeping a diary on this part of the trail except Tamsen Donner, and her diary has never been found, so information is not very reliable. They knew that their situation was critical, so apparently they again decided to send two men ahead to Sutter's Fort for supplies. Lists were made and authorization given:

> *River Truckee Nov. 1, 1846:*
> *I authorize Millford Elliot to purchase for me*
> *or hire 4 work mules & 1 set harness & 3 yoke work*
> *cattle for which I will be responsible on my arrival*
> *in Calif.*
> > *W. M. Foster*
>
> *River Truckee Nov. 2, 1846:*
> *I authorize the bearer Millford Elliot to purchase*
> *for me 6 yoke work cattle & 3 beeves for which I will*
> *pay cash or goods on my arrival in Calif.*
> > *Jacob Donner*

Misfortune struck again when a gun accidently discharged and killed one of the men, William Pike. He left his wife and two children to struggle on toward the mountains and the many difficulties they would encounter there.

The Donner party left the Truckee Meadows in different groups and at different times. The two Donner families were the last to leave. The first groups reached the Sierra Nevada at the end of October and attempted to cross. However, because of deep snow on the ground, a snow storm, and a lack of strong leadership, they returned to Donner Lake. Here they found one cabin that had been built two years before and they built two more. These are the cabins that later emigrants saw and called "Cannibal Cabins" or "Starvation Camp."

The George and Jacob Donner families never reached Donner Lake as a unit; only individual members actually saw the lake. On approaching Alder Creek, approximately six miles from the lake, an axle broke on one of their wagons while descending a short, steep hill. It was snowing, and in trying to shape a new axle the chisel slipped and made a large gash in George Donner's hand. They were near the head of a little valley, so they hurried to the large trees for protection from the storm. They constructed some shelters out of canvas and other materials but did not build cabins.

Hill descending to Alder Creek where
George Donner probably broke the axle
on his wagon.

167

Three and four years later emigrants apparently did not see or know of this camp at Alder Creek. They don't mention it in their diaries, with the one exception:

Two miles brought us to the valley where Donner encamped. 1 mile more brought us opposite to where his cabins were which were situated about 1 mile or 2 from the road on the right side. There were a number of fragments left, but more human bones than anything else.

John A. Markle (1849)

Location of the Donner Camp on Alder Creek
where many of the Donners died.

Here at Alder Creek the Donner party still had hopes of crossing the mountains and were now thinking of leaving the wagons and packing. Milt Elliot was again preparing to leave:

Mr. Elliot:
   Please bring me 5 mules to pack also 4 low priced active ponies suitable for women and children to ride - 200 weight flour - 2 bushels beans - 2 gal salt -

> *3 dollars worth sugar if it can be had on reasonable*
> *terms and a cheese. These mules and horses you may*
> *purchase if expedient if not you will hire them.*
>   *Jacob Donner*
> *(These instructions are in case you return this*
> *winter if you stay till spring perhaps oxen will*
> *be better)*
>   Jacob Donner (1846)

But snows became deeper and there was no help until the first relief party arrived on February 19 of the next year. This was too late for many of them. The two Donner brothers, their wives, some of the children, and most of their teamsters died here at Alder Creek. Of the eighty-seven people in the Donner party, five died on the trail before they reached the mountains, nine died at Alder Creek, thirteen died at Donner Lake, and twelve died attempting to cross the mountains. Also, the two Indians that returned with Charles Stanton died while crossing.

Later, more fortunate emigrants camped near Donner Lake to rest for their climb over the Sierra Nevada. The original trail over the mountains went along the north shore of Donner Lake and then over the summit between old Highway 40 and the Southern Pacific Railroad showsheds. This was a very difficult pass, because of the many large rocks:

> *After a day's travel we came to a rim rock ledge where*
> *there was no chance to drive up, so the wagons were*
> *taken to pieces and hoisted to the top of the rim*
> *rocks with ropes. The wagons were put together again,*
> *reloaded and the oxen which had been led through a*
> *narrow crevice in the rim rock were hitched up and*
> *went on.*
>   Benjamin Franklin Bonney (1846)

In 1846, a party decided to find an easier way and explored the valley to the south of Donner Lake:

> *We spent three days there exploring the mountains to*
> *find a pass where we might make a crossing. A party*
> *of us took our horses and went to the summit and traced*
> *it both ways and finally decided on the place to make*
> *the crossing.*
>   Joseph Aram (1846)

This trail in the valley south of Donner Lake was called the Cold Stream Canyon Trail. It was not a very difficult pass until they were within one thousand feet of the top. Then it became very steep, especially the last three hundred feet. This last section is so difficult that it is hard to believe that the emigrants took wagons and animals up it:

> The road from the Donner Huts has been changed, instead
> of going around Truckee's Lake as formerly, it begins
> to ascend the mountains immediately, being a savings
> of some 4 or 5 miles. The Lake is some 2 miles to the
> right & was described to me by those who visited it as
> a beautiful sheet of clear water about 3 miles long by
> about 1 broad. The ascent to the pass from Donner
> Cabins is about 5 miles over rocks & steep bluffs . . .
> Up, up, we toiled wondering every five minutes how "the
> dickens" ox teams & wagons can get over here, & it is
> a wonder indeed, untill at 3 P.M. arrived at the foot
> of the terrible "Passage on the Backbone." For half
> hour before arriving we could hear the shouts of
> teamsters urging their cattle up the steep, & when we
> were near enough to see through the forest we could
> look up nearly over our heads & see wagons & cattle
> looking like pigmies, & as if almost suspended in the
> air. The "Pass" is through a slight depression in the
> mountains being some 1500 or 2000 feet lower than the
> tops in its immediate vicinity.
>
> As we came up to it the appearance was exactly like
> marching up to some immense wall built directly across
> our path so perpendicular is this dividing ridge & the
> road going to its very base turns short to the right &
> ascends by a track cut in the side of the mountain till
> two thirds up when it turns left again and goes directly
> over the summit. The distance to the top of the pass I
> should judge to be about ½ mile & in this short space
> the elevation attained is somewhere near 2,000 feet.
>   Elisha D. Perkins (1849)

The pass was so steep that people in the meadows below, looking up over the tops of the trees at the summit, experienced an optical illusion. Wagons on the summit or nearing it would look as if they were on top of the trees:

> From the place where we stopped at noon we could see
> the summit across the tops of the tall firs. We were
> very much astonished to see what appeared to be several
> covered emigrant wagons on the top of the trees and
> could not understand how they got there. Only later
> did we realize that the wagons were not on the top of
> the trees but on the highest ridge beyond the trees . . . .
>
> We immediately recognized the difficulty of crossing
> it. The combined efforts of twenty men would hardly
> be sufficient to drive up there. For us it was entirely
> out of the question. The others had used almost the

steepest grade for their crossing. Since no animal
could climb up there all the ox chains had been
fastened together, and when these did not reach from
the base to the summit, a number of tall young firs
had been notched deeply enough that the chains could
be fastened to them. Up on top twenty oxens were
hitched together by chains, one behind the other.
Below, a wagon was fastened to the long line of
chains and young trees, and various ropes were also
tied to the tongue and to the back of the wagon for
purpose of holding it.

                         Heinrich Lienhard (1846)

A yoke of oxen is two oxen, and some used as many as twelve yoke to take
a wagon up this pass:

We put five yoke on a wagon, and had as many with it
as was necessary to keep it from sliding sideways.
Then with five yoke on the summit letting down our
long one hundred and fifty feet rope, and hitched
it with the leaders that were on the wagon, by this
process we succeeded.

                            Joseph Aram (1846)

To make it easier to get the wagons up this steep section a roller was constructed
at the crest of the summit. Some of the oxen were driven to the top and a chain
attached to the wagon below. This made it possible for the oxen to pull on top
on level ground. Sometimes the oxen were also attached to the wagon as helpers:

Our pilot Mr. Greenwood, who had already informed us
that we had arrived in California; advised us to
follow the counsel of our fellow traveler Mr. Judson
Green, who proposes to make a roller, and fasten
chains to the wagons, and pull them over the mountains
with the help of twelve yokes of oxen. I consider it
needless to say that Mr. Green's plan worked admirably,
and in a few days the whole of our party was safely
placed on top of the mountain.

                         Nicholas Carriger (1846)

We passed the highest of the sierra this morning. At
the same we saw the windlass with which the first
emigrants to California drew up their wagons.

                            D. Jagger (1846)

It was snowing . . . . And in order to get the wagon
over the precipitous slopes ten oxen were hitched to
a wagon, then it was driven as far as it could go and
then a chain was attached that worked on a roller on

PROFILE OF

EMIGRANT PASS BETWEEN MT. JUDAH AND MT. LINCOLN, SIERRA NEVADA MOUNTAINS, ON TRUCKEE RIVER ROUTE

EMIGRANT TRAIL TO CALIFORNIA

How the wagons were pulled to the pass:

In September, 1846, the Aram and Carriger Parties are credited as having first located and used this pass. The Carriger Party with Caleb Greenwood as guide built a log roller with pine trees at the lip to act as a bearing for chains connecting multiple yoke of oxen at the crest with a wagon below (or with additional yoke connected directly to a wagon below the crest). The route to this pass was via Cold-stream and Emigration Canyons or via Coldstream Canyon.

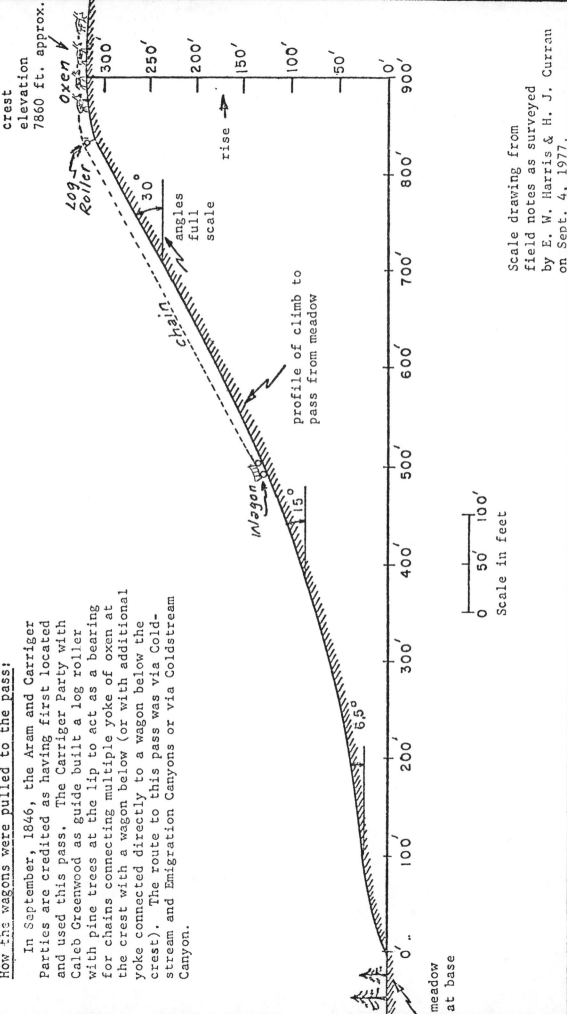

crest elevation 7860 ft. approx.

Log Roller

oxen

Wagon

chain

profile of climb to pass from meadow

angles full scale

30°

15°

6.5°

rise

900 800 700 600 500 400 300 200 100 0'

300'
250'
200'
150'
100'
50'
0'

0'
meadow at base

Scale in feet
0   50'   100'

Scale drawing from field notes as surveyed by E. W. Harris & H. J. Curran on Sept. 4, 1977.

*the top of the mountain. With a man at each wheel
the summit was at last reached.*
                                        Mary Jones (1846)

Emigrant trail at top of Lincoln-Judah Pass (#2 pass).

Cold Stream Canyon Pass was located between Mt. Judah and Mt. Lincoln. The difficulty of ascending the last section of it soon led to the discovery of another pass to the north, by Donner Peak. This third pass was easier than the other two, a gradual ascent to the summit without any particularly difficult sections. The second pass, between Mt. Judah and Mt. Lincoln, and the third, to the north by Donner Peak, are approximately one and one half miles apart. This writer believes that the emigrants heading for both these passes used Cold Stream Canyon to the big bend of the railroad and then used Emigrant Canyon until the trails split approximately two miles from the summits. From the tops of the passes they could look back and see the routes they had traveled:

Our route back could be traced for miles & the
mountains among which we had been winding our way.
                          Elisha D. Perkins (1849)

Emigrant trail near Donner Peak Pass (#3 pass).

Looking down the steep gorge whence we had come, we
bade adieu to its dark avenues, towering cliffs,
sequestered shades, bright waters and melancholy
scenes. We felt a real relief in bidding farewell
to the mountains, valleys, and desert of the great
interior, with its adventure, romance, tragedy,
sorrow, suffering and death - scenes which will
linger in our minds as memorials of our journey
across the plains.

                          John Steele (1850)

The three passes over the Sierra Nevada above
Donner Lake on the Truckee River Route.

#1 - Donner Pass - between old Highway 40
and the Southern Pacific Railroad snow sheds.

#2 - Lincoln-Judah Pass - the steepest
pass where the roller was used.

#3 - Donner Peak Pass - the last pass
opened and the easiest of the three.

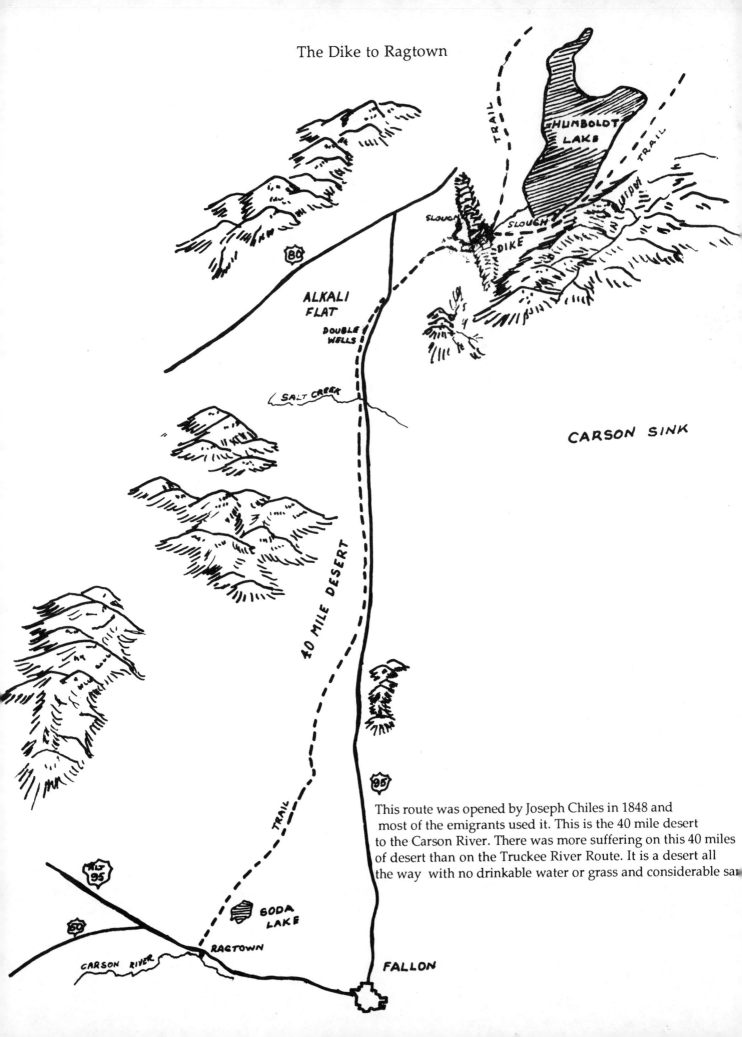

The Dike to Ragtown

HUMBOLDT LAKE

TRAIL

TRAIL

SLOUGH

SLOUGH

DIKE

80

ALKALI FLAT

DOUBLE WELLS

SALT CREEK

CARSON SINK

40 MILE DESERT

95

TRAIL

This route was opened by Joseph Chiles in 1848 and most of the emigrants used it. This is the 40 mile desert to the Carson River. There was more suffering on this 40 miles of desert than on the Truckee River Route. It is a desert all the way with no drinkable water or grass and considerable sa

ALT 95

SODA LAKE

50

RAGTOWN

CARSON RIVER

FALLON

IX. The Carson River Route

From the natural dike to the Carson River it is forty miles, so there is a second Forty Mile Desert. Either way, by the Truckee or the Carson route, the emigrants had forty miles of desert to cross.

The Carson River route was the newer and was used by most of the emigrants in 1849 and 1850. With so many on this route there was great suffering and tragedy. Before entering the desert the emigrants filled everything they could with water and grass:

> Everything that would hold it was filled with water,
> Viz: - Canteens, kegs, gum boots, gum sacks, life
> preservers, coffee pots, buckets (with cover tacked
> over), & our wagon Fisk put in boat or sack shape
> Chadwicks rubber blanket & put in 5 buckets of water.
> Some trains sent ahead men to dig more wells which
> being done they guarded to have the benefit of them.
>   Peter Decker (1849)

Most of the emigrants liked to start late in the afternoon, but some reversed this starting time:

> Twelve o'clock at night started a cross desert - the
> road was good for 20 miles . . . We traveled until
> day light which brought us half way across the desert
> being twenty miles from the slough.
>   W. W. Wixom (1851)

Approximately five miles into the desert they came to what we now call Double Wells. The water in these wells was very poor and most of the stock refused to drink it:

> In about 6 or 8 miles reached salt springs. This
> is verry salt water to salt for horses, - or cattle.
>   Leander Vaness Loomis (1850)

> We came to two wells of water, but not fit for use it
> being verry salty.
>   William H. Kilgore (1850)

> 6 or 8 miles reached Salt Springs - by the springs on
> the desert there is a large lake of salt water, it is
> almost strong enough for brine to save meat with.
>   Dr. Horace Belknap (1850)

Double Wells.

Emigrant trail leaving Double Wells.

The trail ascended a small hill after leaving Double Wells, and soon came to Salt Creek. In wet years this was a difficult crossing:

The first twelve miles of our road this morning was good. Here we reach Salt Creek - or rather a slough from the pools - into the waters of which all the substances, such as alkali, borax, salt, etc., had been thrown together. For some distance the surrounding flats were almost impassable, not swampy as one would understand by the word, but rotten. With great difficulty we passed over this place, wagons sinking to the bed, mules miring, etc.
                                    Jasper M. Hixson (1849)

Salt Creek Crossing.
The emigrants had a difficult time here because of the sticky mud.
The rocks may have been put here by the emigrants to make an
easier crossing.

*In 12 ms we struck salt creek a most disagreeable place.
We crossed this just as the Moon went down. The water
of this place is said to kill stock instantly.*
                                    James A. Pritchard (1849)

179

After crossing Salt Creek, the emigrants traveled over an alkali flat and then came to the beginning of the sand:

> *We entered upon a flat and perfectly bare desert of*
> *4 or 5 miles width by the road & in length run down*
> *12 or 15 to the mountain base on the south. On the*
> *right at the distance of a mile it was bounded by*
> *sand banks. This is level as a lake and appears at*
> *certain seasons to be under water & its lake like*
> *appearance is peculiar when casting the eye over its*
> *extended bosom.*
>
> Peter Decker (1849)

Emigrant trail approaching an alkali flat on the Forty Mile Desert.
After crossing this flat the emigrants found deep sand.

> *After crossing the slough we had a good road for 8 miles*
> *when we came to a point of sand of less than 1 mile but*
> *it gave us a forecast of what we afterwards found for*
> *miles.*
>
> Jasper M. Hixson (1849)

The emigrants were now approaching the half-way mark of their crossing, and they were seeing more and more discarded property and dead animals:

*Started about four o'clock in the morning, weather
unusually cool and the roads good. About ten miles
out the dead teams of 49 and 50 were seen scattered
here and there on the road very soon, however, they
became more frequent and in a little while filled
the entire roadside; mostly oxen with here and there
a horse and once in a while a mule. Wagons, wagon
irons, ox chains, harness, rifles, and indeed all
the paraphernalia of an emigrant's "outfit" lay
scattered along this notorious route, reminding
one of the defeat of some great army. In many
places the teams lay as they had fallen; poor beasts -
they had struggled on over mountains, plains, and
through the sands of the barren desert for days and
weeks with but little or no food, but still with
strength sufficient to make this their last effort
to gain a haven of rest. Good water and plenty of
food lies just beyond; but alas, strength failed
and here they lie, and sad memorials of a grand
crusade to 'the land of gold'. Although dumb brutes
and created for the use of man, I could not help but
deplore their sad fate as there they laid in mute
silence, marking our course through the great desert
they had not the strength to cross.*

John Hawkins Clark (1852)

*The destruction of property upon this part of the road,
is beyond all computation. Abandoned wagons litterally
crowded the way for twenty miles, and dead animals are
so numerous, that I have counted fifty carcasses within
a distance of 40 rods. The desert from side to side
is strewn with goods of every name. The following
articles however, are peculiarly abundant; log chains,
wagons, wagon irons, iron bound water casks, cooking
implements, all kinds of dishes and hollow ware,
cooking stoves and utensils, boots and shoes, clothing
of all kinds, even life preservers, trunks and boxes,
tin bakers, books, guns, pistols, gunlocks, gun barrels.
Edged tools, planes, augers, and chisels, mill and cross
cut saws, good geese feathers in heaps, or blowing over
the desert, feather beds, canvas tents and wagon covers.*

Franklin Langworthy (1850)

*Deep sand which continued for 14 miles I saw 200 wagons
in ½ mile and dead animals so thick you could step from
one to another.*

George Willis Read (1850)

Crossing this same section in 1862, a cattleman wrote:

181

Each side of the road is white with the bones of
cattle and horses that perished in the desert in
crossing to California. Tons and tons of wagon
irons and chains could be gathered along the road.
                                        J. F. Triplett (1862)

Barrel hoops and other iron on the Forty Mile Desert.

Nature has taken care of all this abandoned property, but even today one may
see an occasional rusty bolt or square nail, or sometimes an ox shoe. Barrel
hoops lasted longer than anything else.

   Thousands of animals died on the Forty Mile Desert, thousands of dollars
worth of property was abandoned, and there was great human suffering and
death. The very descriptive John Wood summarizes this destruction and
suffering:

> *We now begin to meet with the destruction of property*
> *and stock; the road being almost lined with wagons,*
> *the dead and dying horses, mules and cattle. We*
> *traveled until 10'clock, when one of the steers*
> *belonging to my mess gave out, and two more belonging*

to other messes.

They were left, and we went to victory, stalking our way through indescribable scenes of suffering and want . . . hundreds of horses, mules and cattle dead, dying and suffering, are laying thick around, and wagons, carts, and carriages line both sides of the road; also, property of all kinds lying in large heaps, such as harness, clothing, tools of all kinds, cooking utensils, trunks and chains. This man who has been selling water here for several weeks, told me that it was estimated by all that there had been left on this plain or desert, this season at least 3,000 wagons and at a low estimate of $3,000,000 worth of property and thousands will yet be left.

But the destruction of property and stock is and will not be all. Hundreds will toil on this far, and then leave their bones to bleach on the Great American Desert, and the worst of it all now is to see, every few hundred yards, the grave of some kind brother, father or mother, and even some who have not been buried, but have probably been foresaken when sick or faint, and left to die and waste away in the winds and rains of heaven.

But the sight of the dead is not so fearful as the living dying. God of heaven! Could human suffering appease thy wrath, the world would soon be forgiven.
John Wood (1850)

Death was a part of the Forty Mile Desert crossing:

A man died near us last night. He was picked up on the desert and brought this far by some gentlemen from Davenport, Iowa. He was left there by his messmates sick, without food or water, and when found, his hands and face were so blistered by the scorching sun that the skin all pealed from them, leaving them as raw as a piece of beef. Poor fellow! When found he was crying in the most excruciating agony for a drop of water to quench his burning thirst. Burning at the stake would be too merciful to the hardened wretches who left him sick and helpless on those burning sands.
Eleazer Stillman Ingalls (1850)

Under mounds lie the dead of 1849 - 50 - 51 - 52 and 53 who perished in passing over . . . Passed a grave with a headboard marked: I. Parks. In memory of Margaret Sept. 19th 1853.
Hozial Baker (1859)

Some experienced a fate worse than death:

> *There were only seven men out of the entire able to*
> *lend a hand. Some were howling for water, and some*
> *threw themselves in a fainting state under the shade*
> *of the waggons . . . I found one of the teamsters*
> *altogether incapable of driving, and, sore against*
> *my grain, had to place him and the two insane men in*
> *the waggons, the latter having become so restless and*
> *outrageous that I was reluctantly constrained to resort*
> *to the disagreeable alternative of tying them down.*
> William Kelley (1852)

Before reaching the Carson River some of the emigrants made a short detour to Soda Lake, where there was a good spring of fresh water:

> *We turned to the left from the road, passed over a*
> *ridge and there found a fresh water spring, also a*
> *salt water lake of about five miles in surcumpherance.*
> *This Lake has a verry high rim or Ridge around it and*
> *had neither inlet or outlet and the water is exceeding*
> *Salty.*
> William H. Kilgore (1850)

> *Turned off about a mile from road to visit a small*
> *salt lake, where we found a very good spring of fresh*
> *water and a sulphur spring. This lake is about three*
> *miles from Carson River; its waters are more salt*
> *than the most salt brine, and its shores are encrusted*
> *with pure salt.*
> Eleazer Stillman Ingalls (1850)

It took most of the emigrants 24 hours to cross the desert:

> *August 28 started on the desert at two o'clock in the*
> *morning and drove through 40 miles in 24 hours.*
> James Mason (1850)

Some made better time:

> *We were just 15 hours crossing from the slough*
> *5 miles below the sink to Carson River.*
> James A. Pritchard (1849)

The Carson River with its large cottonwood trees was a heavenly sight to those weary people:

> *Before we got to the river we were so nearly famished*
> *for water that our tongues were Black and neither could*
> *talk. We got to the river and such water we could not*
> *drink our tongues were so swolen but we burried our*
> *faces in the clear bright water guzeled it us [up] as*
> *best we could then waited a few minutes and guzel again.*

*Before we got through there was a drove of cows came
down on us but we wanted to drink as bad as they did
and laid there and drank with a cow on each side of us.*
                    James Carpenter (1852)

*The first trees large enough to form a shade we had
seen in 1,100 miles . . . Men were seen to rush up,
half crazed with thirst and hunger and embrace these
noble old trees and weep as children, and bless God
for their deliverance.*
                    Jasper M. Hixson (1849)

The emigrants met the river at Ragtown, seven miles west of Fallon,
Nevada on alternate Highway 95:

*This point, on the river, bears the classic name of
Ragtown. The reason for the appellation is because
there are several acres here, literally covered with
rags or clothing, either sound or tattered.*
                    William G. Johnston (1849)

*Rag Town consists of a few shantys built by putting
posts in the ground and then they nail canvas to
them including the roof.*
                    Unknown, Virginia City Fire House Diary

*Ragtown was so named from a party of Californians who
came back with pack train and provisions. First white
man town except Mormon City since Iowa. Number of
tents as store, cooking rooms, etc. 50¢ for a cup of
soup and $1.00 each for 2 biscuits - pushed on to
river where better feed and water could be obtained.*
                    D. A. Shaw (1850)

*Ragtown is well named, being made up of some 50 or
more Pole and Canvas tents. Where can be found all
kinds of vulgar amusements Whiskey & brandy of the
worst possible quality for 25 cents per drink.*
                    Dr. John H. Wayman (1852)

*The traders here buy horses of the emigrants for from
2 lbs. of flour to 10 per head. Such is the destitution.
I saw one horse, saddle and bridle, a very good one too,
sold on the desert for three gallons of water.*
                    Eleazer Stillman Ingalls (1850)

There were unique structures at Ragtown:

*Looking around us we saw the renowned Ragtown, as it
was christened by the emigrants. It consisted of
tattered canvas tents, close to a corral, the like of*

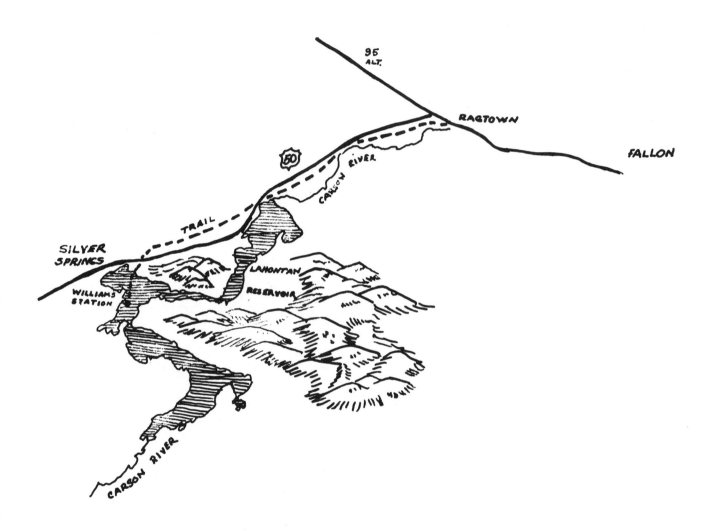

After resting on the Carson River at Ragtown the emigrants followed up the river except for a detour around a very narrow canyon which now bears that name - The Narrows.

which I do not believe could be found on either side
of the Rockies. There was no timber close by and the
practical owner of the town had gone out on the desert
and gathered a lot of rifle barrels and log chains . . .
Gathering the rifle barrels for posts and the ox
chains for rails the enterprising settler built a
stout corral, sufficient to hold any horse or cow
left behind or traded for.

John B. Haas (1853)

The Carson Trail, like the Truckee Trail, had different routes depending on the year and the individual. Leaving Ragtown, the emigrants traveled up the river a few miles and then made a detour to avoid a difficult canyon which is now called the Narrows:

Traveled up the river 8 miles & took over the Bluff
for 14 miles striking the river agane no grass nor
water.

S. M. Jamison (1850)

The remains of Haws Station is on this detour and the trail leading to the river.

Remains of Haws Station and the emigrant trail
on the detour around the Narrows on the Carson River.

Near the river, at the end of this detour, was later built Williams Station. It became well-known as the site where, in 1860, some white men were either justly or unjustly murdered by Indians, which resulted in a civilian army being raised and marched to Pyramid Lake to avenge their deaths. In the ensuing First Battle of Pyramid Lake, the volunteer army was badly defeated. Williams Station was destroyed, but another station, Honey Lake Smiths, was built a short distance from it. Williams Station and Honey Lake Smiths are now under the back-water of Lahontan Dam. In the late 1970's, when the water was very low, the locations of these two were exposed. The location of Honey Lake Smiths was then discovered.

Iron at Honey Lake Smiths Station.
Note the iron from an ox yoke which held the ring to which the wagon tongue or chain was attached.

The emigrants who continued south from these stations passed near the future location of Fort Churchill. They traveled west on the north side of the Carson River, and were soon at the base of a high cliff called Susans Bluff. A romantic version says this bluff was named after Susan, a beautiful Indian

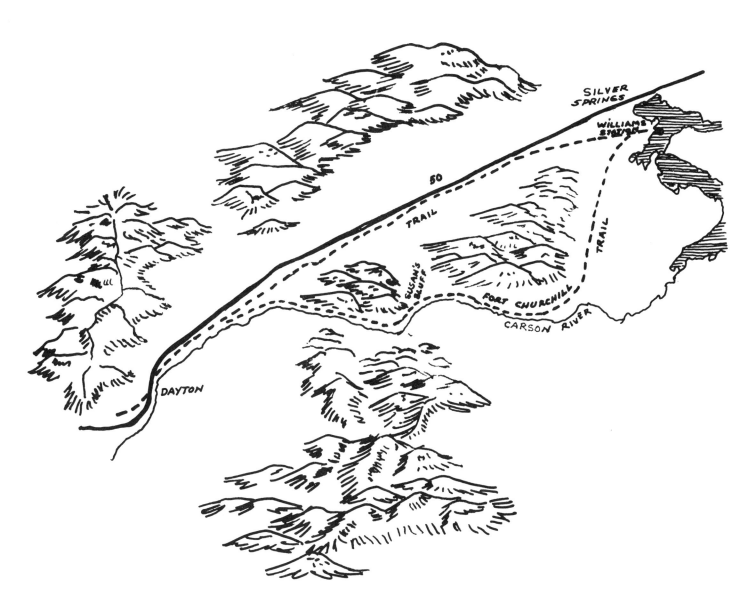

The backwaters of Lahontan Dam cover the location of Williams Station. There were two routes from the station. One route went southwest to the

Carson River, while the other took a straight route west. They rejoined near Dayton.

maiden who chose to leap to her death from it rather than face life without her lover.   There are also other versions of how it received its name:

> *Encamped at the foot of Susan's Bluffs, a high cliff*
> *of rocks, named by myself in 1858, in honor of a young*
> *lady, a former resident of Clarksville, Calif.*
> J. F. Triplett (1862)

> *At its foot are the graves of three emigrants with*
> *a sunken wagon tire at the head of each grave.   The*
> *name of one of the emigrants was Susan.*
> Robert A. Allen Collection

Susans Bluff.

John Williams followed this river route:

> *We drove 14 miles up the river went across a desert*
> *of 12 miles to river - 15 miles on river road -*
> *15 miles up river, crossed it at noon, road rough*
> *and sandy in places. Camped on river - 8 miles and*
> *crossed river - there was a provision at this place.*
> John T. Williams (1850)

Instead of going south after leaving the river by Williams Station, most of the emigrants headed west over a wide open desert with no obstacles except the lack of water. After a few miles travel on the desert they were parallel to the river and could return to it whenever they wanted. The different routes converged at the present location of the town of Dayton, where trading posts were soon established.

Leaving the Dayton area, the emigrants went through Eagle Valley, where Carson City is now located, and then to Mormon Station (Genoa) in Carson Valley. This was a beautiful valley where they could trade or sell stock and rest for the crossing of the Sierra:

> *The road continued along the base of the mountains as if it was seeking an outlet from the most beautiful valley - the valley of the Carson River which here spreads out and forms a most beautiful grazing country . . . The river threads its way down the center of the valley some miles from the road which keeps to the base of the Sierra Nevada Mountains towering more than a thousand feet above our heads . . . . The valley lay before us with grass as high as a horse's back as far as one could see.*
>
> Lemuel C. McKeeby (1850)

> *The most important place is the 'Mormans Station' which is a fortified post where goods are kept for sale at enormous prices.*
>
> Addison Moses Crane (1852)

> *Passed 2 m. from the Mormon Station some hot springs!!!! There must be 2 or 3 hundred of these springs and they form a marsh of 2 or 300 acres, of rushes.*
>
> Byron N. McKinstry (1850)

From Mormon Station, the trail continued along the west side of Carson Valley toward Woodfords, California. There it turned west up Woodfords Canyon, following the West Carson River. The emigrants had a difficult time negotiating this canyon because it was very narrow, the water was swift, and the canyon was full of large rocks:

> *After traveling 4 miles farther we came to the end of the valley, turned to the right, we entered a narrow ravine, bordered on both sides by perpendicular and very high granite rocks. A branch of Carson River passes through this Gorge. The road is very rocky, making it dangerous for wagons, many of which lie by*

Dayton to Carson Pass

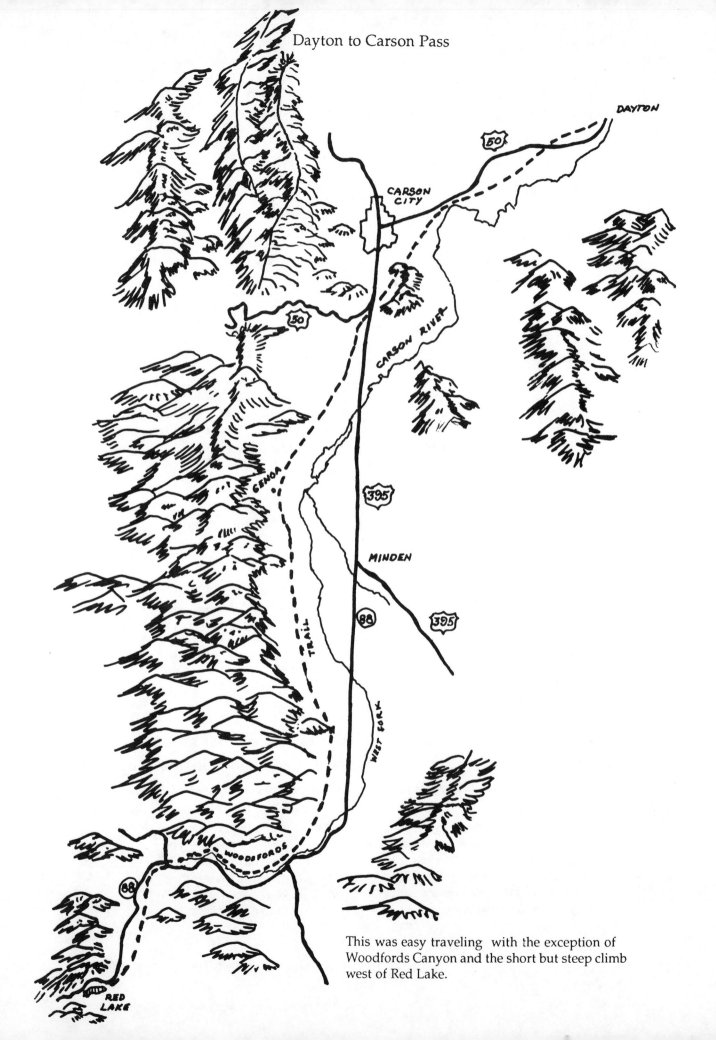

This was easy traveling with the exception of Woodfords Canyon and the short but steep climb west of Red Lake.

*the side of the road broken to pieces. The distance
through the ravine is 4 miles.*
Charles Gould (1849)

Woodfords Canyon and West Carson River.
Called Pass Creek by the Mormons.

A group of Mormons returning to Salt Lake from Placerville, California, pioneered the road through this canyon:

*Here we expect to lay by for several days in order to
work a road through the canyon about four miles and
very bad.*

*A general turnout to work on the road, making fording
places to cross the creek. Considerable digging to do
and rolling rocks out of the way.*
Henry W. Bigler (1848)

Even after this road building by the Mormons, there were plenty of rocks, as the emigrants going up the canyon discovered:

> *Rocks four feet high and so close together [they] fill*
> *the entire roadway. We unhitch our teams, lead them*
> *through and over them to a place of smooth earth, then*
> *go back, pull [off] our coats and lift our wagons from*
> *rock to rock a distance of several hundred yards.*
>   John Hawkins Clark (1852)

> *The river came foaming through it in brawling cascades,*
> *leaving room enough, such as it was, for a mule to travel*
> *along it, but getting more compressed and gloomy as we*
> *advanced . . . The path too, if path it could be called*
> *was unprecedently rugged, both mules and waggons staggering*
> *over confused piles of rocks, where a goat could scarcly*
> *walk with confidence.*
>   William Kelley (1852)

The Mormons named the West Fork of the Carson River through this canyon Pass Creek, and later called the Carson River, Pilot River.

Even with all the trouble to get through this canyon, some of the emigrants found beauty in it:

> *Soon entered into a canon of Pass Creek perhaps the*
> *grandest and most boldly romantic scenery in America*
> *when we entered it & through its length.*
>   Peter Decker (1849)

> *We passed through a Kanyon, or deep hollow. The mountains*
> *on either side arose to the height of 3 to 500 feet. The*
> *scenery wild, romantic, yes sublime, in the highest degree.*
> *4 miles of this road was most decidely the worst road I*
> *ever passed over with a team.*
>   George Willis Read (1850)

> *The scenery of this Canyon, exceeds all I have yet seen*
> *for wild magnificense.*
>   Franklin Langworthy (1850)

After ascending the canyon, the emigrants came to a beautiful little valley, Hope Valley, which was also named by the Mormons:

> *Moved across about one mile and half and camped at*
> *the head of what we called Hope Valley, as we began*
> *to have hope.*
>   Henry W. Bigler (1848)

> *After getting through the Kanyon we entered a valley*
> *several miles in extent at an elevation far above*
> *Carson Valley, and watered by Carson River, which here*
> *but little else than a spring branch.*
>   Madison B. Moorman (1850)

Hope Valley named by the Mormons.

Soon the emigrants reached Red Lake to rest for their short but steep climb to Kit Carson Pass:

> *This is a small lake and is within one mile of the*
> *Summit of the Sierra Nevada. From this Lake to the*
> *summit the Assent is very great, some places being*
> *almost perpendicular.*
> William H. Kilgore (1850)

At the southwest corner of the lake there was only one place to go, and that was up:

> *After refreshing ourselves and teams at the lake, we*
> *clambered up an ascent of about two miles, which is*
> *the most dreaded by emigrants of any upon the entire*
> *land route to California.*
> Franklin Langworthy (1850)

> *Passed a lake on our right just before reaching the*
> *foot of the mountains, the mountain is near 1 mile*
> *high and verry steep and rocky, we might say almost*
> *perpendicular, it Beet anny thing that ever, I saw,*

195

for waggons to pass over, however we came over.
                          Leander Vaness Loomis (1850)

*. . . just ahead was a wall several thousand feet
high which had to be climbed to get out of this
valley. Had we not seen by the trail and the dust
arising from those ahead that others were going that
way we would have come to the conclusion this was
the end of the road . . . It was called the Devils
Ladder.*

                          Jasper M. Hixson (1849)

Southwest corner of Red Lake.
Trail went up center of picture
to Kit Carson Pass.

*A short distance beyond the lake, came to the foot of
the steep, where the trail curled up the formidable pass,
at the foot of which we halted for the night to make
preparations for the undertaking. Had we met such an
ascent in the earlier part of the journey, I fancy we
should have pronounced it insurmountable, and turned
back in despair; but having encountered so many dangerous
places, and overcome so many difficulties, we became*

*inured to hazard and toil, only regarding the greatest
obstacles as merely perplexing, but never impossible;
and as this was the only remaining one, we were resolved
not to be stopped, even if recourse must be had to the
agency of powder. It was not only right up and down,
but leant a little over.*

William Kelley (1852)

At the top a group of Oddfellows left their names on the rocks. The lodge has maintained them and placed a plaque there in honor of these emigrants.

Emigrant's names on Kit Carson Pass
left by a group belonging to the Oddfellows Lodge.

Thus the overland emigrants struggled over various routes. They took the Walker River route to Sonora Pass, the Applegate Trail to the Fandango Pass, the Truckee Trail to the three passes beyond Donner Lake, and, finally, the Carson Trail to Kit Carson Pass. At these crests of the Sierra, with the promised land in sight, the story of their journey through Nevada comes to a close.

David Rohrer Leeper

Bibliography

Allen, Robert A. Collection, Nevada Historical Society, Reno.

Altrocchi, Julia Cooley. *The Old California Trail*. Caldwell, Idaho, Caxton Printers, Ltd., 1945.

Andrews, D. B. *See* Eaton, Herbert.

Aram, Joseph. *See* Kelly, Charles.

Bailey, Mary Stuart. *See* Eaton, Herbert.

Baker, Hozial H. *Overland Journey to Carson Valley & California*. San Francisco, The Book Club of California, 1973.

Bancroft, Hubert Howe. *History of California, 1848-1859*. Vol. 6. Works of Hubert Howe Bancroft. San Francisco, The History Company, Publishers, 1888.

Banks, John Edwin. *See* Scamehorn, Howard L.

Belknap, Horace. *See* Loomis, Leander Vaness.

Bidwell, John. *A Journey to California, a Day-by-Day Record of the Journey from May 18, 1841, to November 6, 1841*. With an Introduction by Herbert Ingram Priestley. San Francisco, John Henry Nash, Printer, 1937.

Bigler, Henry W. *See* Gudde, Erwin G.

Blackburn, Abner. "Diary." Manuscript Collection, Nevada Historical Society, Reno.

Bloom, Henry Sterling. *See* Paden, Irene.

Bonney, Benjamin Franklin. *See* Lockley, Fred.

Brooks, Elisha. *A Pioneer Mother of California*. San Francisco, Harr Wagner Publishing Co., 1922.

Brown, James Berry. *A Journal of a Journey Across the Plains in 1859*. Edited with an Introduction by George R. Stewart. San Francisco, The Book Club of California, 1970.

Brown, John E. *Journey Across the Plains to the Pacific*. By his Daughter - Mrs. Katie E. Blood. Parkersburg, West Virginia, n.d.

Bruff, J. Goldsborough. *Gold Rush, the Journals, Drawings, and Other Papers of J. Goldsborough Bruff, Captain, Washington City and California Mining Association, April 2, 1849 - July 20, 1851*. Edited by Georgia Willis Read and Ruth Gaines, with a Forword by F. W. Hodge. New York, Columbia University Press, 1949.

Buffum, Joseph Curtis. *See* Moorman, Madison Berryman.

Carpenter, Helen McCowen. *See* Coy, Owen Cochran.

Carpenter, James. *See* Eaton, Herbert.

Carriger, Nicholas. *See* Morgan, Dale.

Caughey, John Walton, ed. *Rushing for Gold*. Pacific Coast Branch of the American Historical Association. Special Publication No. 1. Berkeley, University of California Press, 1949.

Chase, Don M. *They Came This Way*. Sebastopol, California, Privately Published, 1973.

Child, Andrew. *Overland Route to California, Description of the Route,* . . . Introduction by Lyle H. Wright. Los Angeles, N. A. Kovach, 1946.

Christy, Thomas. *Road Across the Plains, A Guide to the Route from Mormon Crossing, Now Omaha, Nebraska, to the City of Sacramento, California . . . Compiled from His Personal Observations During the Spring and Summer of 1850* . . . Edited and Cartographically Interpreted by Robert H. Becker. Denver, Old West Publishing Company, 1969.

Clark, Bennett C. *See* Webb, Todd.

Clark, John Hawkins. *See* Eaton, Herbert.

Clark of Virginia, John. *See* Eaton, Herbert.

Cline, Gloria Griffen. *Exploring the Great Basin*. Norman, University of Oklahoma Press, 1963.

Clyman, James. *James Clyman Frontiersman, the Adventures of a Trapper and Covered-Wagon Emigrant as Told in His Own Reminiscences and Diaries*. Edited by Charles L. Camp. Portland, Oregon, Champoeg Press, 1960.

Cole, Gilbert.L. *See* Sawyer, Lorenzo.

Coy, Owen Cochran. *The Great Trek*. San Francisco, Powell Publishing Company, 1931.

Cramer, Thomas, "Journal of Thomas Cramer, 1859." Typescript, Robert A. Allen Collection, Nevada Historical Society, Reno.

Crane, Addison Moses. *See* Eaton, Herbert.

Cummings, Mariett Foster. *See* Eaton, Herbert.

Dawson, Nicholas. *Narrative of Nicholas "Cheyenne" Dawson, (Overland to California in '41 & '49, and Texas in '51)*. With an Introduction by Charles L. Camp. San Francisco, Grabhorn Press, 1933.

Decker, Peter. *The Diaries of Peter Decker, Overland to California in 1849 and Life in the Mines, 1850-1851*. Edited by Helen S. Giffen. Georgetown, California, The Talisman Press, 1966.

Delano, A. *Life on the Plains and Among the Diggings; Being Scenes and Adventures of an Overland Journey to California: With Particular Incidents of the Route, Mistakes and Sufferings of the Emigrants, the Indian Tribes, the Present and the Future of the Great West*. Auburn and Buffalo, Miller, Orton & Mulligan, 1853.

DeWolf, David. *Diary of the Overland Trail - 1849 and Letter 1849-50 of Captain David DeWolf*. Springfield, Illinois, Transactions of the Illinois State Historical Society, 1925.

Donner, Jacob. *See* Hall, Carroll D.

Eaton, Herbert. *The Overland Trail to California in 1852*. New York, G. P. Putnam's Sons, 1974.

Elliot, Milt. *See* Hall, Carroll D.

Farquhar, Francis P. *History of the Sierra Nevada*. Berkeley, University of California Press in collaboration with the Sierra Club, 1965.

Ferguson, Charles D. *The Experiences of a Forty-Niner During Thirty-Four Years' Residence in California and Australia*. Edited by Frederick T. Wallace. Cleveland, Ohio, The Williams Publishing Company, 1888.

Foster, W. M. *See* Hall, Carroll D.

Frink, Margaret A. *Journal of the Adventures of a Party of California Gold-Seekers Under the Guidance of Mr. Ledyard Frink During a Journey Across the Plains from Martinsville, Indiana, to Sacramento, California, from March 30, 1850, to September 7, 1850*. n.p., n.d.

Geiger, Vincent. *Trail to California, the Overland Journal of Vincent Geiger and Wakeman Bryarly*. Edited with an Introduction by David Morris Potter. New Haven, Yale University Press, 1962.

Gould, Charles. *See* Hannon, Jessie Gould.

Gray, Charles. *Off at Sunrise, the Overland Journal of Charles Glass Gray*. Edited with an Introduction by Thomas D. Clark. San Marino, California, Henry E. Huntington Library and Art Gallery, 1976.

Greeley, Horace. *An Overland Journey, From New York to San Francisco, in the Summer of 1859*. New York, C. M. Saxton, Barker & Co., 1860.

Griffen, Helen S. *Trail-Blazing Pioneer - Colonel Joseph Ballinger Chiles*. San Francisco, John Howell Books, 1969.

Gudde, Erwin G. *Bigler's Chronicle of the West, the Conquest of California, Discovery of Gold, and Mormon Settlement as Reflected in Henry William Bigler's Diaries*. Berkeley, University of California Press, 1962.

Haas, John B. "John B. Haas . . . Pioneer Autobiography." Typescript, Robert A. Allen Collection, Nevada Historical Society, Reno.

Hale, Israel F. "Diary of a Trip to California in 1849." *Quarterly of the Society of California Pioneers* 2:61-130.

Hall, Carroll D., ed. *Donner Miscellany, 41 Diaries and Documents*. San Francisco, The Book Club of California, 1947.

Hannon, Jessie Gould. *The Boston-Newton Company Venture from Massachusetts to California in 1849*. Lincoln, University of Nebraska Press, 1969.

Hickman, Richard Owen. *An Overland Journey to California in 1852*. Edited by Catherine White. Missoula, State University of Montana, 1929.

Hixson, Jasper M. *See* Coy, Owen Cochran.

Holliday, J. S. *The World Rushed In, the California Gold Rush Experience*. New York, Simon and Schuster, 1981.

Hulbert, Archer Butler. *Forty-Niners: The Chronicle of the California Trail*. Boston, Little, Brown, and Company, 1931.

Ingalls, Eleazer Stillman. *Journal of a Trip to California by the Overland Route Across the Plains in 1850-1851.* Waukegan, Illinois, Tobey & Company, 1852.

Jagger, D. *See* Caughey, John Walton.

Jamison, S. M. "Diary of S. M. Jamison 1850." *Nevada Historical Society Quarterly* 10:3-26.

Johnston, William G. *Overland to California, a Member of the Wagon Train First to Enter California . . . in the Memorable Year of 1849.* Foreword by Joseph A. Sullivan. Oakland, California, Biobooks, 1948.

Jones, Mary. *See* Griffen, Helen S.

Keller, George. *A Trip Across the Plains.* Foreword - J. A. Sullivan. Oakland, California, Biobooks, 1955.

Kelley, William. *Across the Rocky Mountains, From New York to California: With a Visit to the Celebrated Mormon Colony, at the Great Salt Lake.* London, Simms and M'Intyre, 1852.

Kelly, Charles, and Morgan, Dale L. *Old Greenwood, the Story of Caleb Greenwood: Trapper, Pathfinder, and Early Pioneer.* Revided Edition. Georgetown, California, The Talisman Press, 1965.

Kilgore, William H. *The Kilgore Journal of an Overland Journey to California in the Year 1850.* Edited by Joyce Rockwood Muench from the Original Manuscript Journal of William H. Kilgore. New York, Hastings House, 1949.

Langworthy, Franklin. *Scenery of the Plains, Mountains and Mines: or a Diary Kept Upon the Overland Route to California, by Way of the Great Salt Lake: Travels in the Cities, Mines, and Agricultural Districts - Embracing the Return by the Pacific Ocean and Central America, in the Years 1850, '51, '52 and '53.* Ogdensburgh, J. C. Sprague, Book-Seller, 1855.

Leeper, David Rohrer. *The Argonauts of 'Forty-Nine, Some Recollections of the Plains and the Diggings.* South Bend, Indiana, J. B. Stoll & Company, Printers, 1895.

Leonard, Zenus. *Leonard's Narrative, Adventures of Zenas Leonard Fur Trader and Trapper 1831-1836.* Edited by W. F. Wagner. Cleveland, The Burrows Brothers Company, 1904.

Lewis, John N. *See* Eaton, Herbert.

Lienhard, Heinrich. *From St. Louis to Sutter's Fort, 1846.* Translated and Edited by Erwin G. and Elisabeth K. Gudde. Norman, University of Oklahoma Press, 1961.

Lillard, Richard G. *Desert Challenge, an Interpretation of Nevada.* New York, Alfred A. Knopf, 1942.

Lockley, Fred. *Across the Plains by Prairie Schooner, Personal Narrative of B. F. Bonney of His Trip to Sutter's Fort, California, in 1846, and of His Pioneer Experiences in Oregon During the Days of Oregon's Provisional Government.* Eugene, Oregon, Koke-Tiffany Co., n.d.

Loomis, Leander Vaness. *A Journal of the Birmingham Emigrating Company, The Record of a Trip from Birmingham, Iowa, to Sacramento, California, in 1850.* Edited by Edgar M. Ledyard. Salt Lake City, Utah, 1928.

Loveland, Cyrus C. *California Trail Herd, The 1850 Missouri-to-California Journal of Cyrus C. Loveland.* Edited and Annotated by Richard H. Dillon. Los Gatos, California, Talisman Press, 1961.

Markle, John A. "John A. Markle's Diary." Typescript excerpts in Author's Collection.

Mason, James. *See* Webb, Todd.

Mathers, James. *See* Morgan, Dale.

Maxwell, William Audley. *Crossing the Plains, Days of '57. A Narrative of Early Emigrant Travel to California by the Ox Team Method.* San Francisco, Sunset Publishing House, 1915.

McAuley, Eliza Ann. *See* Eaton, Herbert.

McGlashan, Charles Fayette. *History of the Donner Party, a Tragedy of the Sierra.* With Forword, Notes, and a Bibliography by George H. Hinkle and Bess McGlashan Hinkle. Stanford Univeristy, California, Stanford University Press, 1940.

McGlashan, M. Nona. *Give Me a Mountain Meadow, the Life of Charles Fayette McGlashan (1847-1931) Imaginative Lawyer-Editor of the High Sierra, Who Saved the Donner Story from Oblivion and Launched Winter Sports in the West.* Fresno, California, Valley Publishers, 1977.

McKeeby, Lemuel C. *See* Webb, Todd.

McKinstry, Byron N. *The California Gold Rush Overland Diary of Byron N. McKinstry 1850-1852.* With a Biographical Sketch and Comment on a Modern Tracing of His Overland Travel by His Grandson Bruce L. McKinstry. Glendale, California, The Arthur H. Clark Company, 1975.

McKinstry, George. *See* Morgan, Dale.

Menefee, Arthur M. "Travels Across the Plains, 1857." *Nevada Historical Society Quarterly* 9:2-28.

Moorman, Madison Berryman. *The Journal of Madison Berryman Moorman, 1850-1851.* Edited, With Notes and an Introduction, by Irene D. Paden, Together with a Biographical Sketch of the Author by His Granddaughter Louise Parks Banes. San Francisco, California Historical Society, 1948.

Morgan, Dale, ed. *Overland in 1846, Diaries and Letters of the California-Oregon Trail.* Two volumes. Georgetown, California, The Talisman Press, 1963.

Ogden, Peter Skene. *Peter Skene Ogden's Snake Country Journals 1827-28 and 1828-29.* Edited by Glyndwr Williams, With an Introduction and Notes by David E. Miller and David H. Miller. London, The Hudson's Bay Record Society, 1971.

Orvis, Andrew. *See* Geiger, Vincent.

"Pacific Tourist Guide 1879." *Nevada Historical Society Quarterly* 6:5-7.

Paden, Irene. *The Wake of the Prairie Schooner.* New York, The Macmillan Company, 1943.

Page, Elizabeth. *Wagons West, a Story of the Oregon Trail*. New York, Farrar & Rinehart, Inc., 1930.

Perkins, Elisha Douglas. *Gold Rush Diary*. Edited by Thomas D. Clark. Lexington, University of Kentucky Press, 1967.

Platt, P. L. *Traveler's Guide Across the Plains Upon the Overland Route to California*. By P. L. Platt and N. Slater. Introduction by Dale Morgan. San Francisco, John Howell-Books, 1963.

Pringle, Virgil. *See* Morgan, Dale.

Pritchard, James Avery. *The Overland Diary of James A. Pritchard from Kentucky to California in 1849*. With a Biography of Captain James A. Pritchard by Hugh Pritchard Williamson. Edited by Dale L. Morgan. Denver, Old West Publishing Company, 1959.

Rader, Iva. "Iva Rader's Story." *Nevada Historical Society Quarterly* 6:13-22.

Read, George Willis. *A Pioneer of 1850, George Willis Read, 1819-1880*. Edited by Georgia Willis Read. Boston, Little, Brown, and Company, 1927.

Reed, James Frazier. *See* Hall, Carroll D.

Richardson, Caroline. *See* Eaton, Herbert.

Royce, Sarah Bayliss. *A Frontier Lady: Recollections of the Gold Rush and Early California*. Foreword by Katherine Royce. Edited by Ralph Henry Babriel. New Haven, Yale University Press, 1932.

Sawyer, Mrs. Francis. *See* Eaton, Herbert.

Sawyer, Lorenzo. *Way Sketches Containing Incidents of Travel Across the Plains from St. Joseph to California in 1850 With Letters Describing Life and Conditions in the Gold Region*. Introduction by Edward Eberstadt. New York, Edward Eberstadt, 1926.

Scamehorn, Howard L., ed. *The Buckeye Rovers in the Gold Rush, an Edition of Two Diaries*. Edited with an Introduction by Howard L. Scamehorn. Athens, Ohio, Ohio University Press, 1965.

Shaw, D. A. *Eldorado or California As Seen by a Pioneer, 1850-1900*. Los Angeles, B. R. Baumgardt & Co., 1900.

Shaw, Reuben Cole. *Across the Plains in Forty-Nine*. Edited by Milo Milton Quaife. Chicago, R. R. Donnelley & Sons Co., 1948.

Shepherd, J. S. *Journal of Travel Across the Plains to California and Guide to the Future Emigrant*. Published by Mrs. Rebecca Shepherd, 1851. Reprinted January 1945.

Smith, Charles W. *Journal of a Trip to California. Across the Continent from Weston, Mo., to Weber Creek, Cal. in the Summer of 1850*. Edited and With an Introduction and Notes by R. W. G. Vail. New York, The Cadmus Book Shop, [1920.]

Smith, Jedediah Strong. *The Southwest Expedition of Jedediah Smith: His Personal Account of the Journey to California, 1826-1827*. Edited with an Introduction by George R. Brooks. Glendale, California, The Arthur H. Clark Company, 1977.

Snodgrass, R. H. P. *See* Eaton, Herbert

Snyder, Jacob R. "The Diary of Jacob R. Snyder Written While Crossing the Plains to California in 1845." *Quarterly of the Society of California Pioneers* 8:224-260.

Soule, Andrew. "The Journal of Andrew Soule and Phoebe Twerwilliger, His Aunt." Typescript, Robert A. Allen Collection, Nevada Historical Society, Reno.

"Southern Pacific Bulletin 1958." *Nevada Historical Society Quarterly* 6:9-12.

Stabaek, Tosten Kittelsen. *An Account of a Journey to California in 1852.* Translated by Einar I. Haugen. Northfield Studies on Records, 1929.

Staples, David Jackson. *See* Hannon, Jessie Gould.

Steele, John. *Across the Plains in 1850.* Edited with Introduction and Notes by Joseph Schafer. Chicago, The Caxton Club, 1930.

Stewart, George Rippey. *The California Trail, an Epic with Many Heroes.* New York, McGraw-Hill Book Company, Inc., 1962.

Swain, William. *See* Holliday, J. S.

Thissell, G. W. *Crossing the Plains in '49.* Oakland, California, 1903.

Thornton, J. Quinn. *The California Tragedy.* With a Foreword by Joseph A. Sullivan. Oakland, California, Biobooks, 1945.

Triplett, Joseph F. "The Diary of Joe F. Triplett," ed. by Edna B. Patterson. *Nevada Historical Society Quarterly* 2:3-14.

True, Charles Frederick. *Covered Wagon Pioneers.* Edited by Sally Ralston True. Madison, Wisconsin, College Printing Company, 1966.

Turnbull, Thomas. "T. Turnbull's Travels from the United States Across the Plains to California." From the *Proceedings of the State Historical Society of Wisconsin for 1913,* pp. 151-225. Madison, Published for the Society, 1914.

Utter, Jo. *See* Altrocchi, Julia Cooley.

Virginia City Fire House Diary. Robert A. Allen Collection, Nevada Historical Society, Reno.

Ward, Harriet Sherrill. *Prairie Schooner Lady, The Journal of Harriet Sherrill Ward, 1853.* As Presented by Ward G. DeWitt and Florence Stark DeWitt. Los Angeles, Westernlore Press, 1959.

Ware, Joseph E. *The Emigrants' Guide to California* . . . St. Louis, J. Halsell, 1848. Reissued in 1932 by Princeton University Press.

Wayman, John Hudson. *A Doctor on the California Trail, the Diary of Dr. John Wayman from Cambridge City, Indiana, to the Gold Fields in 1852.* Edited by Edgeley Woodman Todd. Denver, Old West Publishing Company, 1971.

Webb, Todd. *The Gold Rush Trail and the Road to Oregon.* Garden City, New York, Doubleday & Co., 1963.

Webster, Kimball. *The Gold Seekers of '49, a Personal Narrative of the Overland Trail and Adventures in California and Oregon From 1849 to 1854.* With an Introduction and Biographical Sketch by George Waldo Browne. Manchester,

New Hampshire, Standard Book Company, 1917.

Wilkins, James F. *An Artist on the Overland Trail, the 1849 Diary and Sketches of James F. Wilkins*. Edited by John Francis McDermott. San Marino, California, The Huntington Library, 1968.

Williams, John T. "1850 Diary." Robert A. Allen Collection, Nevada Historical Society, Reno.

Williams, Velina. "Oregon Pioneer Association." *Transaction of the Forty-Seventh Annual Reunion of the Oregon Pioneer Association* - Portland, June 19, 1919. Portland, Oregon, Chausse-Prudhomme Co. Printers, 1922.

Wixom, W. W. "W. W. Wixom's Journal." Photostat copy, Robert A. Allen Collection, Nevada Historical Society, Reno.

Wood, John. "Along the Emigrant Trail, Beginning an Authentic Account of Pioneer Days as Recorded by John Wood in His Diary While Crossing the Country to California in 1850." *Motorland* 23: (Dec.) 6-9+; 24: (Jan.) 9-11+, (Feb.) 14-16+, (Mar.) 12-15+, (April) 14-16+.

Yager, James Pressley. "The Yager Journals: Diary of a Journey Across the Plains." *Nevada Historical Society Quarterly* 13:(No. 1) 3-19, (No. 2) 18-39, (No. 3) 26-48, (No. 4) 26-52; 14:(No. 1) 26-54, (No. 2) 33-54.

[The Youth's Companion.] *Our Country: West*. The Companion Series. Boston, Perry Mason Company, 1902.

Index

Toana Range, 72
Triplett, J. F., (quote) 182, (quote) 190
Truckee, Chief, 27
Truckee (California), 27, 161, 162
Truckee High School, 162
Truckee Lake, *see* Donner Lake
Truckee Meadows, 154, (quotes) 157-159, 166, 167
Truckee River, 27, 28, 49, 85, 103, (quote) 133, 140, 144, 148, 150, 151, (quotes) 152, (quote) 154, (quotes) 156-157, (quote) 161, 162, 164, 166
Truckee River Route, 27, 108, (quote) 138, 140, 144, (quotes) 161-162, (quote) 164, 175, 177, 187, 197
True, Charles F., (quote) 45
Turnbull, Thomas, (quote) 129, (quote) 138
Tuscarora Range, 88

Unknown River, *see* Humboldt River
Upper High Rock Canyon, (quote) 118
Utter, Jo, (quote) 145

Valley of Fountains, *see* Ruby Valley
Verdi, 27, 161
Virginia City Fire House Diary, (quote) 89, (quote) 185
Vya, 121

Wabuska, 25
Wadsworth, 140, 152, 154, 156
Waldo Relief party, 151, (quote) 152
Walker, Joseph, 13, 15, 16-20, 21, 23, 24, 26-27
Walker-Bonneville party, 15, 23, *see also* Bonneville party
Walker Lake, 14, (quote) 15, 17, 18, 19, 20, 26, 79, (quote) 80
Walker Pass, 19
Walker River, (quote) 15, 18-19, 25
Walker River Route, 26, 197
Ward, Harriet S., (quote) 55-56, (quote) 100, (quote) 125, (quote) 148, (quote) 156
Ware, Joseph E., 43, 44
Warm Springs, 74
Wasatch Mountains, 69, 70, 85
Washoe County Golf Course, 159
Wayman, John H., (quote) 138, (quote) 185
Weber Reservoir, 25

Webster, Kimball, (quote) 103, (quote) 106, (quote) 108, (quote) 116
Wells, 21, 23, 61, 63, 69
Wendover, 69
West Carson River, *see* Carson River
West Humboldt Range, 24
West Walker River, *see* Walker River
Westfall, Susan, (quote) 148, (quote) 150
Wild Horse Pass, 24
Wilkins, James F., (quote) 32
Williams, John T., (quote) 190
Williams, Velina A., (quote) 56, (quote) 95, (quote) 97, (quote) 102, (quote) 110, (quote) 132
Williams Station, 140, 188, 191
willow bridge, (quote) 157
Wilson Canyon, 25
Wind River, *see* Little Truckee River
Winnemucca, 14, 23, 47, 97, 102
Wixom, W. W., (quote) 34-35, (quote) 60, (quote) 63, (quote) 177
Wood, John, (quote) 37, (quote) 41, (quote) 42, (quote) 43, (quote) 72, (quote) 76, (quote) 143, (quote) 182-183
Woodfords (California), 191
Woodfords Canyon (California), (quote) 191, (quotes) 193-194

Yager, James Pressley, (quote) 94, (quote) 142
Yerington, 18
Yosemite Valley, 18, 19